OBSERVING SPIRIT

OBSERVING SPIRIT

Evaluating Your Daily Progress on the Path to Heaven with Gurdjieff and Swedenborg

PETER RHODES

Edited by
Jody Perkins and Ruth Zuber

Chrysalis Books

©2005 by Peter Rhodes

Library of Congress Cataloging-in-Publication Data

Rhodes, Peter, 1944–
Observing spirit: evaluating your daily progress on the path to heaven with Gurdjieff and Swedenborg/Peter Rhodes ; editors, Jody Perkins and Ruth Zuber.
p. cm.
ISBN 0-87785-316-9
1. Spiritual life. 2. Fourth Way (Occultism) 3. Swedenborg, Emanuel, 1688–1772. I. Perkins, Jody. II. Zuber, Ruth. III. Title.
BL624.R44 2005
204'.4--dc22
2004030999

Credits: Quotations from *Psychological Commentaries on the Teaching of Gurdjieff and Ouspensky* by Maurice Nicoll are excerpted with permission of Red Wheel/Weiser, Boston, MA, and York Beach, ME, USA. To order please call Red Wheel/Weiser at 1-800-423-7087.
The Scripture quotations contained herein are from the New Revised Standard Version Bible, copyright ©1989 by the Division of Christian Education of the National Council of the Churches of Christ in the U.S.A., and are used by permission. All rights reserved.
Chrysalis Books is an imprint of the Swedenborg Foundation, Inc. For more information, contact:
Swedenborg Foundation Publishers
320 North Church Street
West Chester, PA 19380
or
http://www.swedenborg.com

CONTENTS

ACKNOWLEDGEMENTS

I would like to thank:

My wife Roxanne, whose support is invaluable to me.

Frank and Louise Rose who first gave me the opportunity to talk to a group about using the teaching of G.I. Gurdjieff, P.D. Ouspensky, and Maurice Nicoll in applying the truths of religion, especially those revealed by Emanuel Swedenborg, to our daily life.

Valerie Rogers, who coerced me into leading weekly "Work" groups on the above subject, and who, along with others in the group, made sure these talks were taped.

The Work group, which met regularly for over four years, and especially Ruth Zuber, who transcribed my lecture tapes. She also found the quotes that I had paraphrased and sometimes misquoted. She arranged and edited the transcribed material and arranged for others to do additional work on the rough transcription. I feel a little like the waiter who is thanked for a fine meal prepared by a great chef. Ruth has been and is a great chef in this regard.

I would also like to acknowledge Jody Perkins who reorganized, edited, and improved my wording and terminology to be more accessible to a broad audience, and also Tom Bramel, her husband, who helped and supported her in the work.

Lisa Hyatt Cooper took on the arduous task of updating the biblical quotations and updating and retranslating the original Latin of Swedenborg's quotations to be most current and correct. For this I am very thankful.

Finally I would like to thank Jonathan Rose, Ray Silverman, Sarah Headsten, Catherine Kerst, and Mary Ambrosio who read, critiqued, and gave valuable suggestions for improvements to the book, resulting in a more valuable final product.

No play, no symphony, and no meal are the result of any one person. All original material and its formation come from God. I am pleased to have been permitted to be a part of this process and thank all those mentioned above who contributed so much.

PREFACE

Spiritual work is separating from the noise and clamor of outer life in order to move towards something quieter. It is an effort to elevate one's self toward something that is already there but that is much finer than an ordinary and external way of life.

— *Peter Rhodes*

*I*f you are like me, you have at different times found the goal of spiritual development inspiring and mystifying.

For me, the hope of becoming a better person can be strongest when I am already feeling at peace. When I am praying and sense the Lord's presence, for instance, it is easy for me to see that I am on the right path. I can review my shortcomings and renew my commitment to making improvements in the future.

Yet there are also times when my spiritual optimism waivers—such as after I have given in to a temptation and regret doing so. At such times, I can look at what I have done and fear the worst for my spiritual future. I can also feel confused: just a little while ago I was committed to improving, so why did I give in to the temptation? Is my spiritual life actually getting better or worse? How do I proceed from here?

Useful direction came to me when I encountered Peter Rhodes' method of spiritual growth. His approach is broad, encompassing concepts ranging from the theological to the very practical. It is also flexible enough to address the gamut of spiritual experiences. Practicing this method has helped me understand the ups and downs of my spiritual life and gain confidence regarding my efforts and progress, even during the times I could easily feel most discouraged.

Peter Rhodes' approach, as described in this book, has helped many people. If you are searching for spiritual advancement, his method may prove helpful to you as well.

Peter Rhodes' method brings together two systems for spiritual development, one system from the East and one from the West. Each will be more fully described a little later. Here it is important to note several of the primary, fundamental principles that these two systems share.

- *Everyone has the capability of making progress along his or her unique path.* Each one of us has the potential to live a better spiritual life, if we choose to do so.
- *Although active participation in the world is desirable, progress is made by directing effort inward.* Spiritual growth is a personal pursuit. We must seek to change our-selves instead of trying to change the external world, or other people, directly.
- *Study is necessary.* New knowledge is potentially useful, whether it concerns a greater understanding of divine revelation or greater mastery of a practical spiritual skill.
- *Honest examination of the life one is living is also necessary.* We must carefully examine our actions, thoughts, and intentions so that we can more easily distinguish what is good in our lives from what is not good. Only after we have examined our lives closely can our minds open up to consider new possibilities for thinking and acting.
- *Efforts must be made to turn away from or put aside what-ever is not good about the way one is living.* This can be done by using techniques that enhance our awareness of our spiritual states, for example, or by trying to obey the Ten Commandments in both letter and spirit.

Together, these principles provide a foundation for spiritual awareness and growth. Each principle is developed in more detail in the two systems that Peter Rhodes combines.

Now let's examine each of these systems in turn, beginning with the system from the East known as "The Work."*

---

*When the term "Work" is capitalized throughout this book, it specifically refers to the Gurdjieff method.

The Work (referring to "work on oneself") is a complex system of ideas, encompassing both cosmological concepts and specific views as to how human psyches develop and function. It was brought to the West early in the twentieth century by Georges Ivanovitch Gurdjieff. Although many specifics regarding Gurdjieff's early life and his discovery and mastery of the Work are uncertain, some basic facts are reasonably well established.

Gurdjieff was born about 1874 in Alexandropol and raised in Kars, Armenia, in a region of great racial, cultural, and religious diversity. His father was Greek, his mother Armenian. Gurdjieff was raised an Orthodox Christian (Russian or Greek), and even though his family was poor, he studied to be both a priest and a physician. He took a great interest in mechanical things and the innovations in science and technology newly arriving from the West. He also had a fervent need to understand the meaning of life; and when his many inquiries to religious and scientific experts around him failed to provide satisfactory answers, he turned to books. Through his diligent reading, he came to believe that the truth he wanted might once have been known and might be preserved somewhere in ancient traditions still being maintained in another part of the world.

So Gurdjieff the young man set out to find this truth. He traveled and studied for roughly twenty years. His adventurous searching took him to various places in the Middle East, central Asia, India, and northeast Africa. It is thought that Gurdjieff studied with quite a number of religious and spiritual groups, including Sufis and yogis.

Gurdjieff returned to the West with the intention of teaching what he had learned. He first tried to do this in conjunction with existing groups and then began teaching on his own, in Moscow, about 1913. The Work (which also became known by other names, such as the Fourth Way and the System) defies easy categorization and summary, although parallels with both Christianity and Buddhism have been noted.

According to the Work, in the course of growing up, we become focused on the outside world. We learn by imitating what others do. We tend to define ourselves by what we observe in the world around us and how we interact with it, and we learn to seek happiness by trying to control events there. We arrive at adulthood and become effectively able to operate in the world in many ways, but our capability for functioning has been compromised too, because we have emphasized the development of certain mental functions over others. Certain aspects of our awareness are limited, and we often misuse our energy.

However, as adults, we have the potential to develop in a qualitatively different manner. While we maintain our functioning in the world, we can also turn more of our attention and effort inward and learn to achieve more balanced mental functioning (between our thinking and feeling, for example). A better internal balance in turn brings a sense of internal wholeness, individuality, authenticity, and vitality. A heightened awareness develops, and energy can be focused and used more effectively.

A distinguishing feature of the Work is its abstract, symbolic, and metaphorical style of expression. Key ideas are explained in terms of energy, force, the nature of "impressions," and the opposition of real and illusory experiences. Progress can be viewed as raising the quality of one's consciousness, or "level of being," to a higher level. Ordinary states of consciousness are characterized as sleeping or mechanical, while more aware states of consciousness are described in terms of being awake and free. In doing the Work, we can experience "shocks," "take aim," cultivate "magnetic center," and "remember ourselves."

The Work provides practical techniques oriented toward developing self-awareness and accepting the truth of what we actually experience. The Work also acknowledges the difficulty of doing these things.

By the time of Gurdjieff's death in 1949, his ideas were becoming known in Europe and North America, and his teachings continued to spread thereafter throughout the world. Today there are centers of study in the United States, the United Kingdom, France, and many other countries. Spread of the Work was partly due to Gurdjieff himself, who, at the start of the Russian Revolution, moved to the Caucasus, where he established his Institute for the Harmonious Development of Man. In 1922, Gurdjieff moved the institute to Fountainbleau, near Paris. Following a serious injury in an automobile accident in 1924, he turned to writing. His books (which are often allegorical) include *Meetings with Remarkable Men* and *Beelzebub's Tales to His Grandson*. Gurdjieff closed the institute in 1933 but continued to teach in Paris, New York, and other places.

Dissemination of the Work in the West is also attributable to the teaching and writing of several of Gurdjieff's students. The most notable, for our purposes, are two rough contemporaries of Gurdjieff: Piotr Demianovich Ouspensky and Dr. Maurice Nicoll.

P.D. Ouspensky (1878–1947), a Russian philosopher and journalist, met Gurdjieff in 1915. Immediately appreciating the power of Gurdjieff's ideas, Ouspensky studied earnestly, applied Work principles to his own life, and became a colleague of Gurdjieff. Ouspensky moved to London in 1921 and began lecturing on the Work late in that year.

At one of Ouspensky's first London lectures, Maurice Nicoll (1884–1953) initially learned about the Work. So struck was he with the ideas he heard, Nicoll soon arranged to study directly with Gurdjieff at his institute at Fountainbleau.

At the time he met Ouspensky, Nicoll had been practicing as a psychologist in London for some years. A medical doctor (born in Kelso, Scotland) who had studied Freud's and Jung's then-new theories of psychology in Vienna and Zurich and who had served in field ambulances and hospitals during World War I, Nicoll was becoming a pioneer in psychology in his own right. He developed new methods of treating victims of shell-shock and authored one of the first books summarizing Jung's theory of dream analysis (*Dream Psychology*). His decision to study the Work intensively required him to turn down Jung's invitation to be his primary advocate in England.

Following his year at Gurdjieff's institute, Nicoll returned to London, resuming his psychological practice and his studies with Ouspensky. Years later, with Ouspensky's permission, Nicoll began teaching the Work, and eventually he gave up his psychology practice (in 1939) in order to concentrate on these efforts.

Nicoll's subsequent writing on Work concepts and psychology reflected his dedication to Christianity and his general interest in spiritual matters. He had been raised in a religious family; his father was a Presbyterian minister who later adopted a literary career. When young, Nicoll became a devoted Christian; he never felt comfortable, however, with the way Christianity was taught to him, stressing fear of evil more than love of God. As a young man, Nicoll read widely from theological and spiritual literature, including the Bible; literature related to the Gnostics, the NeoPlatonists, and Sufis; and the writings of Meister Eckhart, Jakob Boehme, and Emanuel Swedenborg.

Nicoll relates Work concepts to Christian ideas such as the commandment to love the neighbor as oneself and many of Christ's other sayings, in his extensive series of papers published in the multi-volume *Psychological Commentaries on the Teaching of G.I. Gurdjieff and P.D. Ouspensky*. In *The New Man: An Interpretation of Some Parables and Miracles of Christ*, Nicoll sought to show that the teachings in the Gospels concern the raising of humanity's "level of being" to a higher, less violent state. In addition, Nicoll's books discuss many core concepts in the Christian theology described by Emanuel Swedenborg.

And so, we now turn to Swedenborg's theology, for it is the second system of development employed in Peter Rhodes' method of spiritual growth.

Emanuel Swedenborg (1688–1772) was born into a wealthy family in Stockholm, Sweden. His father was a devout

Lutheran clergyman; his mother came from a family with significant interests in the mining industry. When Swedenborg was still very young, the family moved to Uppsala so that his father could accept a professorship of theology at the university there; his father later would become a bishop.

Swedenborg was well-educated, both formally and informally. At home, discussion of a wide range of political, scientific, philosophical, and religious issues was encouraged. Even when very young, Swedenborg often found himself contemplating spiritual matters. He accepted the Lutheran theology taught to him and enjoyed the opportunities he had for discussing theological matters with clergy, and a family friend also encouraged Swedenborg's interest in religions other than Lutheranism.

Swedenborg attended the University of Uppsala, concentrating his studies in the fields of mathematics and natural science. This choice was made at a time of considerable tension between science and religion. Lutheranism had been the official religion of Sweden for more than a century, and for some years before Swedenborg's birth, there was much debate as to whether the church should remain the final arbiter on academic subject matters. Even though freedom of inquiry was granted to nontheological departments before Swedenborg began his university studies, debate over the policy energetically continued.

After graduating, Swedenborg traveled to Europe to further his studies of science and mathematics. He lodged with various artisans—such as a watchmaker, a cabinet maker, and an engraver—assisting them and learning their trades. He developed a number of inventions ranging from the practical and industrial (including devices for improving mining operations) to the highly theoretical (for example, designs for an airplane and a submarine).

In 1715 Swedenborg returned home and for a time worked as an assistant to the inventor Christopher Polhelm. Soon Swedenborg's family was ennobled, and he began serving in

Sweden's parliament; a few years later he attained an appointment as assessor to Sweden's Board of Mines. Swedenborg also continued his independent scholarly work, publishing a number of scientific and philosophical treatises. By the mid-1730s, he was a prominent expert in mining and one of the most pre-eminent philosophers in Europe.

Swedenborg's research turned to finding the seat of the soul in the body (a not-unusual scholarly pursuit at that time). He studied anatomy, physiology, and psychology, including the brain and the nervous system; but as his investigations progressed, Swedenborg came to look more and more to theology and less and less to physical science for answers to his questions.

This period also marked a personal spiritual crisis during which he had a series of significant dreams and visions that often moved him emotionally or offered him spiritual insights. Two visions of Christ, in 1744 and 1745, introduced and clarified Swedenborg's commission to record and publish the theology revealed to him.

Consequently, Swedenborg abandoned his search for the soul, cut back his civil service (he resigned from the Board of Mines but kept his position in Sweden's parliament), and concentrated his efforts on Bible study and theological writing. He made no attempts to preach or to organize a new religious sect. His many theological books cover a wide number of subjects and include *Heaven and Hell*, *Charity*, *Divine Providence*, and *True Christianity*. He wrote in Latin and used publishers in London and Amsterdam, where freedom of the press was greater than in Sweden. For the most part, he humbly published his theological books anonymously, signing his name only to those volumes published near the end of his life.

According to Swedenborg, each person on earth lives simultaneously in two worlds: one natural (or physical), the other spiritual. Every soul is a unique creation, born into the natural world in a state of innocence. As we grow older, we become more and more responsible for our choices between doing what is good and doing what is not good. Upon reaching adulthood, we are spiritually "rational" beings, possessing freedom to choose between good and evil. At death, we leave our earthly bodies behind and live on in the spiritual world, where, often after going through a process of preparation, we move on as we desire, eventually finding a home in either heaven or hell. The decisions we make after death will reflect how we have made our conscious spiritual decisions here on earth.

Spiritual growth ("regeneration") is the increased choosing of a life of good rather than one of evil. The process can be described in terms of how we prioritize four basic loves—of the self, the world, the neighbor, and the Lord. Certainly, a good spiritual life involves appropriate care for ourselves and our material lives, or appropriate loves of the self and of the world. But if we let a love of the world or of ourselves inappropriately control our desires (through material greed, for example, or a desire to have power over others solely for the sake of dominating them), we will not progress spiritually, because we are viewing and experiencing the world selfishly, valuing events only according to how they affect us personally. The more regenerate a person is, the stronger will be his or her just and compassionate love for the neighbor and his or her love for the Lord (or for doing the Lord's will). Because the Lord, through divine providence, continually provides each person with what is required for that individual to grow closer to him, our potential for regeneration is ever-present and continual.

Two distinctive aspects of Swedenborg's theology concern Bible interpretation. First, Swedenborg provided a system for understanding many books of the Bible on two levels, one literal, the other internal or spiritual. Depending upon the exact passage, the spiritual sense may be fairly obvious or seem quite obscure. Second, Swedenborg's theology characterizes the Lord as knowing and benevolent—perfect wisdom and love. Biblical depictions of the Lord as angry or vindictive are viewed as true in the sense that at times he appears that way to us, while behind that appearance is also the reality that the Lord never actually experiences anger or acts vengefully. Our experience of the Lord as angry can be seen as analogous to that of a child perceiving a caretaker as angry in certain situations, when in fact the caretaker is acting lovingly but expediently (by grabbing the child and pulling him out of harm's way, for example).

After Swedenborg's death in 1772, devoted readers organized the first groups of followers in Sweden, London, and Philadelphia. Eventually, a religion was established, the Church of the New Jerusalem or the New Church. At the present time, there are congregations in various locations throughout the world, and Swedenborg's theological writings are available (in whole or in part) in more than twenty modern languages.

Peter Rhodes, a life-long Swedenborgian, first encountered the Work when a friend gave him a copy of Ouspensky's *In Search of the Miraculous*. His first response to the Work was similar to Ouspensky's and Nicoll's—immediate and profound resonance. Most impressive initially were Ouspensky's description of ordinary life as mechanical and the practical techniques he described for transcending automatic reactions.

This introduction to the Work in Peter's early adulthood ended a period of considerable searching. Peter Rhodes was born (in 1944 in Saginaw, Michigan) into a family long-established in Swedenborgianism. When he was young, his family moved to Bryn Athyn, Pennsylvania, and he attended Swedenborgian schools. He received his bachelor's degree and then worked as a probation officer and as a teacher. He married and began a family. But despite the fact that he was leading a useful life that was rewarding in many ways, he was also developing a deep need for something more; he realized that he accepted the teachings of the New Church but did not feel a personal connection with them.

Peter's quest for deeper meaning led him to many books on psychology and spirituality. He found many interesting concepts and made an especially significant discovery with one of Jiddu Krishnamurti's ideas. Krishnamurti said, in effect, that all anxiety is nonacceptance of what is. Peter attempted to use this idea and discovered that, when trying to be more accepting of life events, he did experience a reduction in anxiety. This experiment proved for him that an important possibility was real—the possibility that there existed theoretical truths about internal experience that could be applied successfully in daily life.

It was not until he read Ouspensky's book, however, that Peter believed he had found a systematic method with general practicality. He continued studying the Work, first through Ouspensky's books and then Gurdjieff's, and subsequently by participating in a Gurdjieff group. Peter next discovered Nicoll's books. By practicing the techniques he learned, he found that the Work indeed had much application to his family life and also to his professional life as he earned a master's degree in counseling psychology and worked as a federal probation officer specializing in psychiatric cases.

When he was nearing the end of reading Nicoll and wondering what he would study next, Peter came to a statement by Nicoll referring interested readers to the interpretation of the Old Testament presented in Swedenborg's *Arcana Coelestia*. Astonished, Peter turned back to Swedenborg's writings and the Bible and found that for the first time he understood them.

With time, Peter realized that Work ideas, especially as expressed by Nicoll, functioned like a translator, illuminating the ways in which Swedenborg's theology and the Bible had application to his own life, his own spiritual states. Swedenborg's works and the Bible had always told him *what* to do (love the neighbor and the Lord, etc.) and *why* he should do it (because the Lord is love, etc.), but the *how* of applying his religion to his life came from the Work.

Excited about his discovery, Peter began sharing Work ideas and books with friends, many of them Swedenborgian. Interested friends convinced him to lead a series of classes one winter. In these weekly classes, Peter explained Work concepts, read passages from Swedenborg, the Bible, Nicoll, and other sources, and shared his own experiences. Each class included a homework task for participants to practice and report on the following week.

Audiotapes of Peter's first and second series of lectures were transcribed and published in *Aim*, his first book, and then in *Aim: The Workbook*. The present book is adapted from his third series of classes.

Peter retired from probation work in 1997. He still lives in Bryn Athyn and works as a counselor using psychological and spiritual principles, and he does occasional public speaking. He is still exploring spiritual books and practices new to him. This he regards as an ever-expanding way of exploring and experiencing his spiritual life while remaining deeply committed to Swedenborgianism.

Like the pursuit of many worthwhile endeavors, the process of spiritual development described in this book is challenging. This process takes effort, and there are times when spiritual enlightenment about oneself is not a particularly pleasant experience. But the rewards can be substantial.

After studying Peter's method and practicing the tasks, I more often experience life in the fullness of the present, rather than being preoccupied with my unchangeable past or unknown future. It is easier for me to see my true intentions and to listen to other people and appreciate the goodness in them. I can also see more options for dealing with life events, behave more in accordance with my true values, and pay better attention to the subtle thoughts and feelings through which the Lord directs me.

I offer good wishes to each of you as you strive to make improvements in your spiritual life.

Jody Perkins
Rockville, Maryland

HOW TO USE THIS BOOK

This book discusses concepts and provides tools appropriate for the spiritual growth of adults (not children or adolescents). Since each chapter builds upon previous material, it is best to begin with chapter 1 and move on from there.

Each chapter provides at least one specific task for the reader to practice. It is desirable to practice each of the tasks, because they are a primary means for learning about your current spiritual state and for becoming aware of your progress. And because the Work stresses that anyone practicing it should verify its teachings for him- or herself, each task provides a new opportunity for doing this.

A person can benefit greatly from reading this book and doing the tasks alone. One benefit to using the book individually is that you can work at your own pace, concentrating on one task for longer than another if desired.

However, students of the Work often find it more productive to form groups of up to ten people who can commit to meeting weekly to discuss their reading and to share their experience of doing the tasks. Such groups can offer valuable support and fellowship.

Mutual trust and caring are developed when meetings are run in a structured way: meetings should begin and end on time, run for an hour to an hour and a half, and permit no eating or drinking. Since maintaining a proper tone is important, it is helpful to follow these guidelines:

- Participants sit in a circle, so that every participant can see and hear everyone else.
- Participants do not interrupt or speak out of turn.
- Participants do not offer criticism or give advice.
- Each participant can feel free to "pass" if he or she chooses not to speak.
- Participants do not use abusive language or bring up divisive topics.

- Participants speak only for themselves and do not use the given name of anyone while sharing.
- Participants keep everything said in a meeting confidential.

Meetings run best when one person acts as a leader, to facilitate meetings as inconspicuously as possible while still helping to maintain order. The leader takes a turn reporting on his or her task experience (just like other participants) and does not judge, admonish, or critique remarks. If the group so desires, leadership can rotate from meeting to meeting.

The format of successful spiritual-growth groups has been as follows:

- *Introduction.* The leader introduces him- or herself and states that the purpose of the meeting is to apply spiritual principles to the participants's everyday lives.
- *Hellos.* Going around the circle, participants take turns briefly answering the implied question "How are you?" (This is not a time for reporting task experiences.)
- *Meditation, prayer, or other exercise.* The leader spends a few moments directing the group in a prayer or other exercise designed to quiet the mind and let go of worldly concerns.
- *Task reports.* Going around the circle, participants take turns reporting on their experience of doing the task for the previous week.
- *Reading.* The leader spends ten minutes or so, depending upon the time available, on a reading. Readings can come from Nicoll, Gurdjieff, Ouspensky, Swedenborg, or the Hebrew or New Testaments.
- *Discussion of new task.* The leader, who has read the next chapter ahead of time, describes the task to practice over the coming week. (Other participants will read that chapter as homework while practicing the task.)
- *Closing thoughts.* Going around the circle once more, participants share any additional thoughts.

- *Closing prayer.* The Lord's Prayer is said, with participants holding hands if the group desires.

Whether you choose to use this book as part of a group or individually, reading the text and practicing the tasks can help you more fully explore the spiritual path the Lord has provided for you.

OBSERVING SPIRIT

CHAPTER 1
Where We Are and Where We Want to Go

We are here only to contend with ourselves. So thank others
who provide you with the opportunity for doing so.
— G.I. Gurdjieff

There are many different ways we might describe our
spiritual states and how they change. Let's begin by
imagining that the process of spiritual growth is like a journey
that takes us away from relatively selfish lives toward lives that
are more loving to others and more open to the Lord's
influence.

To begin any journey successfully, we need to know at least
two things—where we are and where we are going.

Let's say you are flying a plane from Philadelphia to what
you thought was the promised land of San Francisco. The
plane takes off, and then there is a storm. You are pushed off
route by miles and miles. When you are forced to land, you
find yourself in a field in some small town.

Fortunately for you, you brought the perfect, up-to-the-
minute map. This map has everything, every road, every
detour, every path. But is it of any use to you? No, because
you don't know where you are!

Before you can use the map to get to where you want to
go, you have to locate your present position. You might look

around for signs. Let's say that you find the "Harleysville Shopping Center." Well, now you have narrowed it a bit. When you see signs on two crossing roads saying "Route 63" and "I-78," then you've got something you can look up on the map! Find Harleysville on the map with those intersecting routes and you know where you are. Now the map is useful because you know where you are. You can see which direction you want to go.

On any journey, you are going to have to switch back and forth between using your map and looking at reality. You may think, "Now I am on Route 63. What should I look for? Oh yes, I'm looking for I-78." Your attention must constantly go back and forth between checking the map and checking reality.

Traveling spiritually in the right direction requires a similar process of checking. What does reality indicate about my present position? Where am I on the map?

In matters of spirit, divine revelation is the ultimate map, one the Lord gave us to guide our spiritual journeys and to inspire us toward better spiritual states. Revelation provides all the general and all the specific information we might ever need.

But some of us have trouble understanding how to apply the details to our lives, and that is where the system of personal development called the Work can help us. Compared with the perfect map offered in divine revelation, the map provided by the Work is like one a friend might sketch on the back of an envelope so that we can find our way to the ball park. The Work can help us greatly in understanding where we are located on the Lord's ultimate map, determining which direction is the correct one to aim for, and planning out our next moves.

While revelation inspires us, in order to make real progress on our spiritual journeys, we must do what the Work can help us to do. We must pay attention to how we respond to things around us and within us, so that we see where we actually are spiritually. And we must aim our efforts at improvement in the correct direction on a daily basis.

First Steps and Basic Principles

As explained in the preface, the Work is a program of spiritual practice that was first introduced by G.I. Gurdjieff and further developed by his disciples, P.D. Ouspensky and Maurice Nicoll. The first step or phase of the Work is locating where you are spiritually, in actuality, using *noncritical* self-observation. To do this, you must observe your thoughts and feelings while trying to give up attitudes that say "it shouldn't be this way."

As an example, suppose that I am experiencing jealousy. Noncritical observation sees the jealousy for what it is and stops there. But if I notice that I am experiencing jealousy, I may also be thinking, "I shouldn't be experiencing this" or "I could be experiencing something else." Noncritical observation lets go of this kind of judgmental thinking about experiences and just recognizes what the experience is—in this case, "I am experiencing jealousy." That's it. It just is. Observe noncritically, like an experimental scientist noting what occurs during an experiment. Whatever you experience is just an experience.

After you begin observing yourself noncritically and you get a better idea of what kinds of spiritual states you are experiencing, it is important that you accept where you are. Suppose you are on a trip and you aren't exactly sure where you are, but you believe you are in San Francisco. If the evidence shows that you are in Harleysville, you may say, "But I don't want to be in Harleysville! I want to be in San Francisco." It doesn't matter what you used to believe or what you want; Harleysville is where you are if it checks out in reality and on the map.

Another basic Work principle is that each of us often experiences different mental/emotional states rather than one unified state continually. One moment you are happy; the next moment you may be angry, jealous, or depressed. The part of you that goes on a diet may not be the same part of you that later reaches for a doughnut. You cannot count on yourself to act the same at all times. The state you are in when you make one decision is not necessarily connected to another state you may experience before or after that one.

We are, however, inclined to call each of our states "I, myself." But the Work teaches that, because of the many states we actually experience, we are more like a multiplicity of "I's" rather than just one "I."

Making progress spiritually requires gathering together states (or "I's") that *are willing* to grow spiritually or work. We can call these "Work I's." One example of a Work I is "Observing I." Once we non-judgmentally accept the states we're observing, we start to see a distinction between "positive" and "negative" I's or states. The words *negative* and *positive* are definitions or descriptions, not value judgments.

Work I's are positive states. Positive thoughts and feelings are loving toward the Lord or the neighbor, or they are appropriately loving of the self. Positive states can be happy, a feeling of contentment, for example, or an emotion like joy, or a feeling of gladness at the joy of another person. When we have a serene feeling of trusting the Lord, that is a positive state. Positive emotions can also be sad, as when a loved one dies and you are grieving; that is love grieving. Fear, when there is a genuine danger, is a positive emotion.

Negative states are self-centered and not loving; they see and experience the world from how it affects only the self. Hatred is a negative emotion. Happiness can be a negative emotion if its motivation is selfish, such as if we experience happiness when we hear of the misfortune of another person. We can even say that excessive anxiety, when there is not a genuine danger threatening us, is negative, because we are not being loving to ourselves. Other negative emotions are anger, resentment, and self-pity.

When we Work, we learn to develop our Work I's, and we also learn to refuse to entertain negative states or negative I's.

Another key principle in the Work is non-identification. Simply put, although we experience many different positive and negative states, non-identification holds that we are not *any one* of those states. When anger is present, we feel angry; we think angry thoughts; we may even say, "I am angry." *But we are not the anger.* We just have the anger within us at that time.

A crucial goal, therefore, is to Work toward "non-identification" in the way we perceive ourselves and others. When we experience a negative emotion or thought, we do not need to attribute it to ourselves or make it our own. We do not need to justify it. Rather, we can simply observe it and know that we are not that state. The state is merely with us. Maurice Nicoll explained how non-identification moves us forward on our spiritual path:

> Now supposing such a man begins to observe himself in the light of the teaching of this Work and begins to notice what he says and how he behaves and occasionally begins to wonder why he says these things and always behaves like that—such a man is beginning to observe himself and through self-observation begins not to identify with himself. This man, this woman, has begun to pass into a more internal person, [namely,] himself [or] herself.[1]

With regard to other people, the Work teaches that, when someone does something negative or displays certain compulsions, we need not attribute those traits to him or her any more than we identify ourselves with a negative emotion. That person is not that negative trait, although he or she may have that negative for a time.

It is very important that we do not attribute positive or negative states to ourselves or to others.

1. Maurice Nicoll, *Psychological Commentaries on the Teaching of Gurdjieff & Ouspensky* (Boulder, Colo.: Shambhala Publications, Inc., 1984), 800. All quotations taken from this text are reprinted by permission of Red Wheel/Weiser.

Spiritual Growth Activates a Higher Mind

Now that we have a basic introduction to the Work, let's look at the contribution that Emanuel Swedenborg makes to the process of spiritual growth.

Swedenborg wrote that every person has a spiritual mind, a rational mind, and a natural mind:

> Most people do not know that every individual possesses an internal level, a rational level, and a natural level [of the mind], and that these three levels are quite distinct and separate from one another—so distinct in fact that one can be at variance with another. That is to say, the rational level, which is called the rational self, can be at variance with the natural level, which is the natural self; indeed the rational self is able to see and perceive evil that is in the natural, and if it is a genuine rationality, is able to correct it. . . . Before these two have been joined together we are unable to be whole or to experience the serenity of peace, since the one is in conflict with the other.
> — *Secrets of Heaven* §2183[2][2]

Our natural minds use all sorts of worldly knowledge to manage our physical lives. We use knowledge in our natural minds when we dial a telephone, read a book, play the guitar, use a software program on our computer, recall the name of the president in 1924. This kind of worldly knowledge is not in itself either good or bad; it can be used for either purpose.

Also within the natural level of our minds are various states of thought and feeling that can be either selfish or good. For example, if you were born with a patient disposition, then patience would be a natural good of yours. You didn't have to "earn" your patience by Working; it is characteristic of you without conscious effort.

---

2. As is customary in Swedenborgian studies, the numbers following titles refer to paragraph or section numbers, which are uniform in all editions, rather than to page numbers.

With regard to the selfish loves or states within our natural mind, or our lowest level of being, the Work collectively refers to these as "IT." Within IT, for example, are our negative I's. When we learn not to identify with our negative emotions, such as jealousy or anger, then we begin to experience negative states as separate from who we are.

Above the natural level of our minds is the rational level, which can perceive differences between our negative I's and better states. Our rational minds can see what is fair, true, and good in a way that the natural minds cannot. Within our rational minds are our Work I's, our states or loves that are willing to grow spiritually.

Higher even than the rational level is the internal or spiritual level of the mind, which is closer to heaven and the Lord.

When we grow spiritually, we come to see and act more from our spiritual or rational minds and less from the selfish parts of our natural minds. We are better able to see the difference between good states and bad states in ourselves. We are better able to use an Observing I and act from our better states that are good and refrain from acting from negative I's that are always selfish.

The process of spiritual growth involves Work and the Lord's help. With these, everything selfish in the natural mind that cannot serve the higher minds becomes quiescent. We become passive to IT in the sense that we do not act from our negative I's. Then the rational or spiritual mind rules, and the natural mind uses the knowledge at its disposal to serve the higher minds.

I stated earlier that divine revelation is the ultimate map on our spiritual journey. Now that we have been introduced to some basic concepts of the Work, we should take a brief detour to see how the Bible provides us with signs as to how to proceed on our journey.

Emanuel Swedenborg taught that many passages in the Hebrew and New Testaments describe religious truths on different levels. Some passages tell a story on one level, while at the same time, on a different level, they also describe the kinds of states that exist in our natural, rational, and spiritual minds.

In the following passage in Ezekiel, the Lord describes the process of taking people out of one land and bringing them into another land that he has prepared:

> I will take you from the nations, and gather you from all the countries, and bring you into your own land. I will sprinkle clean water upon you, and you shall be clean from all your uncleannesses, and from all your idols I will cleanse you. A new heart I will give you, and a new spirit I will put within you; and I will remove from your body the heart of stone and give you a heart of flesh. I will put my spirit within you, and make you follow my statutes and be careful to observe my ordinances. Then you shall live in the land that I gave to your ancestors; and you shall be my people, and I will be your God. I will save you from all your uncleannesses, and I will summon the grain and make it abundant and lay no famine upon you. I will make the fruit of the tree and the produce of the field abundant, so that you may never again suffer the disgrace of famine among the nations. (Ezekiel 36:24–30)[3]

Let's interpret that passage as a metaphor for our spiritual journey. Implied in the Lord's promise is the idea that we are not yet in the promised land. Spiritually, we now live in the land where there is famine, drought, reproach, and filth.

Now we might not think that we live in such a land. But we are there whenever we feel overly or unnecessarily afraid, angry, jealous, anxious, guilty, or regretful—in other words, whenever negative states are active within us. We live in such

---

3. The Scripture quotations contained herein are from the New Revised Standard Version Bible, copyright © 1998 by the Division of Christian Education of the National Council of the Churchs of Christ in the U.S.A., and are used by permission. All rights reserved.

a land when we see and act from our selfish loves in our natural minds, our IT's.

There is nothing wrong with being in the stage we are in now, since to observe or know where we are is the early part of any journey. Being where we are now is a necessary part of the trip. So is looking at reality and checking our locations on the map. We have to be *here* before we can get to where we want to be.

We are told in the Work to use "objective, noncritical, nonjudgmental" observation on ourselves. The Work also says that before we begin to Work, negative states in us are active a lot of the time. We are not supposed to think, "I shouldn't be anxious; I shouldn't feel covetous; I shouldn't be angry." The fact is we *will* feel those negative emotions. The good news about finding where we really are is that this is a good and necessary stage in our journey toward where we want to be. It is much better to find out where we really are than to dream that we are better people than we are, even if it does not feel as pleasant. At least when we know we are in a bad place, we are motivated to move!

When we can observe our negative states for what they are and get to know them well, we can start to change on the basis of having that knowledge.

Evaluating States of Being

It is not as easy to distinguish between different states as one might suppose, but that is what we are trying to do. In distinguishing between negative I's and Work I's or good states, there are many things we can consider.

We can examine content, for instance, to evaluate a state or clarify a motive. If we are thinking contemptuous things about someone, we can be pretty sure the content of our state is negative rather than positive. If we are talking critically about someone behind her back, we might guess that it is not a Work I talking.

But let's say you are feeling generous and want to give your neighbor a present. You find something they can use in their garden, and you give it to them. Then your neighbor forgets to thank you, and you get angry!

Before you got angry, you might have thought the impulse to give your neighbor a gift was a good Work I. Indeed, your original impulse may have been a good (or positive) one, and then your state changed to anger only when your neighbor forgot to thank you.

Then again, your motivation for giving the gift to your neighbor may have been a negative one—a love of being loved or love of reputation that had an opportunity to enhance itself and be considered a good neighbor. With observation, you can see your true motivation. In fact, if your neighbor had said, "Oh, that is just what I need. Thank you!" you might have gone on thinking your impulse was a good impulse even when it wasn't.

Though sometimes difficult, it is important to be able to tell the difference between a negative emotion and a positive emotion. If we experience sorrow (a positive emotion), it might be very close to self-pity (a negative emotion). We have to distinguish between the two, and that is more difficult than distinguishing between an upset and tranquillity. It might be difficult to tell the difference between a sincere desire to do something for somebody and the desire to do something for somebody for the sole reason that that person will like us. These desires seem very similar.

We want to gain finer observation. It is not just thinking about observing that is required, but *actually* observing, which is very different.

One method for distinguishing Work I states from negative states involves listening to the stream of words in our heads. This often tells us a great deal about our present state.

If the words babble on with no effort and no attention, they have nothing to offer you in terms of spiritual value. They are usually "bumper-sticker" thoughts—ideas that just appear in dyads of good-bad, yes-no, black and white, etc. Even though we each potentially may experience different states of consciousness, the monologue in our heads usually is operating on the relatively low level of yammer. If we pay attention to this talking, we will find that it has nothing new to tell us. It is hugely negative, and it puts us up high and other people down low. But, by being conscious of this mindless chatter, we may be able just to dismiss it or turn it off, like a radio, or turn it down low enough so we can ignore it. Sometimes the monologue may even stop just because we listen to it.

To elevate our consciousness to a higher level takes effort and attention, a desire or willingness to be there. The rational is a higher and more internal level of our mind than the one we usually respond to all day long, which is the natural level with all its selfish loves and negative concerns.

We have to quiet that part of the natural mind and try to wake up to the other higher levels of ourselves.

Contrast is very important to perception and learning. We need contrast so that we can see our different states. For instance, in order to see a joyous state, we might first sink down into a state of depression for a time.

The Ten Commandments provide us with a certain contrast. Thou shalt not do so and so, the Lord says. He is saying that to people who are incapable of refraining from doing all those things all the time. Don't interpret the commandment as the Lord's saying, "Now that you know you shouldn't do it, I expect you to never do it again!" I imagine any of you who have raised children know that you do not just tell them not to do something once, and that is all that is needed. In fact, you probably never had the experience of telling your children once and that being enough!

So why does the Lord say, for example, "Thou shalt not bear false witness"? He knows you are going to do it anyway. Perhaps he commands us to give the opportunity to see that we *do* lie, and then we might think to ourselves, "Oh, yes, I shouldn't be lying!" Unless we have the experience and awareness of lying, we do not have a total knowledge of what should not be done and of what actually *is* being done. We can't overnight be completely done with that fault right now; rather, although our aim is not to lie, we observe that we *do* lie, and after having gained that knowledge, we find our aim is to be separated from that lying.

According to the Work, a person "should not express a negative emotion." What does this mean? It does *not* mean that we should suppress emotions or rationalize them. Rather it means that we should not *act from* negative emotions.

Negative emotions can be acted upon in obvious and not-so-obvious ways. If I open my refrigerator door and see that I am out of milk and react by cursing about the situation, I would obviously be acting upon a negative emotion. On the other hand, suppose I keep quiet upon opening the refrigerator door but make a face at my wife, and, when she asks me what is wrong, I say, "Nothing!" in a sarcastic voice, I would be expressing my negative emotion too. (If instead I could say calmly, "I wish we had some milk," I would succeed in "not expressing my negative emotion.")

Even though we are told not to express negative emotions, we still do. The saying merely reminds us, "This is what I need to Work on."

There are different ways to Work when you are experiencing a negative state. The goal is to divide your attention from your negative thought or emotion. You can focus on your hand using the practice called "sensing" (putting your attention on a spot or pressing until you can feel sensation there and then sustain it as long as you need to). You can pray. Or you can use some other tool like "stop thought"—turning off the monologue going on in your head. If you still hear it, stop believing it or ignore it. You work any way you know how to work.

Gurdjieff stated, "We are here only to contend with ourselves. So thank others who provide you with the opportunity for doing so."[4] This quote really covers it. Who do you work on? Yourself only! You are here only to contend with yourself. Constantly, negative thoughts want to say, "Yes, but. . . ." and argue about everything including the concept of the Work. That is just the way IT is. However, the Work always points the arrow back at you. No matter what reaction you have to any bad thing anybody else does, what you need to work on is your own reaction. Contend with the state within you.

When do you Work? Now! Just when you are about to express (that is, act upon) a negative emotion or even when you are in the middle of expressing it, *that* is when you remember *not* to express a negative emotion. You get to do some Work using effort and attention. You Work when you are about to do something in word or deed or seriously entertain a thought that is in *any* way injurious to another person. Of course, IT won't want to work now because IT doesn't ever want to work at all and always suggests working later. But now is the time to work.

When you work on yourself, you develop some ability to refrain from expressing negative emotions. So, there you are contending with yourself, and you may notice that other people are not in the Work or they are not doing their Work at that time. If they freely express negative emotions or they blame you for something or they have no objection to their own negative state and may even think it is just great, in that situation what do you get to work on? Yourself! Work on your reaction to all of it. That is called "the burden of the Work," namely, to tolerate the negative manifestations of others *without irritation*. Irritation isn't a heavy or furious emotion; it's just a constant judging of other people, whether their faults be slight or great.

---

4. Samuel Copley, *Portrait of a Vertical Man: An Appreciatioin of Doctor Maurice Nicoll and His Work* (London: Swayne Publications, 1989), 56.

So you get to contend with yourself one more time. Of course, IT will say things to you like, "Doesn't anybody else have any responsibility for Working?" The Work says, "No." You are here to Work only on your own irritation.

What does it mean to Work on irritation or frustration? Does it mean to be without any irritation? What does it mean not to express negative emotions, even though you realize you are still going to express negative emotions? It means that you don't *believe* the negative messages in your head. You don't pay attention to them. You don't entertain these kinds of thoughts as being true or being your own or as being necessary. You start to separate from them and see them as something you must Work on, to separate further from them (or get some distance from them) because *they are not you.* You apply everything you have learned in the Work or from divine revelation to that feeling of irritation. You cannot indulge it, act from it, or allow yourself to enjoy it.

As a wise old teacher of mine used to say, "You can let a bird land on your head, but don't let it build a nest there." Negative thoughts can show up univited but don't entertain them or let them stick around.

Spiritual Remembering and Spiritual Forgetting

Can you remember a time from your childhood, going to a refrigerator and finding a favorite drink? As you drank the liquid, you wanted that taste to stay with you forever. Perhaps you closed your eyes as you tasted that delicious beverage and you wanted to make that taste a part of who you were.

You may also have had the experience of tasting something that did *not* taste good. Perhaps you spit it out. You didn't want that taste to be a part of you, so you got rid of it. You didn't let it come in to you or become a part of you.

On a more spiritual plane, consider these quotes concerning the Lord's remembering and forgetting:

He is ever mindful of his covenant. (Psalms 111:5)

And I will not remember your sins. (Isaiah 43:25)

The Lord remembers by continually keeping his covenant in mind. Picture the Lord's covenant with us as his bringing renewal and goodness into our lives as we acknowledge him and avoid doing things that we know are wrong. In contrast, we have the image of the Lord letting go of certain thoughts, as in *I will not remember your sins.*

We too can remember and forget in ways that are good. For example, we may want to forget (or let go of) a bad state or negative I. Perhaps someone affronts you in some way and you have a negative response; but you want to forego that response and just forget it. What do you do? You try to access a higher state by Working. For example, if you can "stop thought" successfully, you may forget why you are angry. Although that same negative voice will try to remind you of the transgression, you will forget why you are angry if you can elevate your thinking and fill your mind with some appreciation of that person for something he or she has done in the past. Use any of the tools outlined in this book for changing your state, and you will allow the Lord to help you go into forgetfulness or forgiveness of whatever the other person did.

The point is this: If you intend to Work and you fill your mind with something higher than yourself, it helps you to forget or give up the connection with the lower negative state. It helps you to remember the Lord's covenant with you.

The important step is to be alert to negative thoughts and emotions. Once you realize that you are experiencing a negative I, immediately begin the Work to separate yourself from your negative reaction. As Working becomes a regular part of your spiritual renewal, you will weaken your identification with automatic negative responses. Maurice Nicoll wrote about our condition:

When you have realized that you cannot help doing something, you will realize that other people cannot help doing something and you will no longer feel this fatal criticism, this contempt, that underlies so many people's psychology. This will give you a right basis to begin to have relationship in the Work-sense to other people. . . . Now a man who begins to realize his own difficulties in the Work will no longer blame other people. . . .[5]

✣

The Task for Chapter 1

List ten negative emotions IT has and from which you wish to be free.

List emotions you actually experience or have previously experienced and from which you sincerely wish to be set free. If you feel there was any use in a certain state, then don't write that one down. List only those emotions you feel sure were negative emotions. And if you find that you only have one negative emotion, that is okay, but the task is to write down ten negative emotions IT has that you don't want.

These are traits or states that your father, mother, grandfather, or grandmother may have given you, that you didn't ask for, but are often in you. These inclinations include emotions you don't own and also those you have made your own over time.

---

5. Nicoll, *Commentaries*, 782.

CHAPTER 2

Progressing in the Work

We must work the works of him who sent me while it is day;
night is coming when no one can work.

— *John 9:4*

Chapter 1 compares the process of spiritual growth to a
metaphorical trip. We need to know where we are and
where we are going.

In order to see where we are, however, the Work tells us
that we must first wake up.

Waking Up

When you begin to Work, you start to wake up. You become
more aware of your reactions, in both thought and deed, to
people and situations.

Unfortunately, when you wake up, you do not find yourself
in the spiritual equivalent of San Francisco or Nepal, even if
that's where you were dreaming that you were. You may have
thought you were already at your destination, but instead you
find you are actually in the city dump, sound asleep. So, after a
little while in the Work, your life is not as comfortable as it
used to be. You are not as happy with yourself as you used to
be. But although you see that there are many negatives in you,

the fact that you see them is good. If you are in a bad place spiritually, it is far better to be awake and aware than to be asleep imagining you are in a good place. Your growing state of wakefulness is very important.

Swedenborg sometimes described our spiritual states in terms of wakefulness and sleep. He also interpreted waking and sleeping images in the Bible ("the Word") as descriptions of spiritual states:

> The person who has not been regenerated is like a dreamer. One who has been regenerated is like someone who is wide awake. In the Word natural [physical] life is likened to sleep and spiritual life to wakefulness.　　— *True Christian Religion* §606

> A person who learns truth and lives by it is like someone who wakens from sleep into consciousness. . . . Natural [physical] life viewed in itself, apart from spiritual life, is nothing but sleep. On the other hand, natural life that has spiritual life within it is consciousness. The only way to obtain this kind of life is by means of truth, which comes into its light and its day-time when we base our lives on it.
> 　　— *Apocalypse Revealed* §158

You will understand why Swedenborg wrote these things if you observe yourself in a negative state. When you are negative, your head may be down, your eyes blurred, your forehead furrowed. You are concentrating on whatever event you think made you negative. You are focused on how another person didn't say hello to you or how someone interrupted you or how your boss didn't value the report you delivered. You cannot see anything else going on in the world, and your relationships are frozen. If you observe closely, you will see that you are in a state that has an unconscious, unreal, or sleep-like quality to it.

With some effort, perhaps you will find you can wake up. When you do this, you will realize that awakening from sleep is not just a symbolic description but a real change in state and that there is a definite qualitative difference between being spiritually asleep and being spiritually awake.

You cannot become a fully spiritual person instantly. There is a period during which you will go in and out of wakefulness and sleep.

By observing yourself objectively, you will notice that sometimes you are identifying with your negative state, feeling "at one" with your negative thought or emotion. Perhaps you are looking at things through a false or selfish perspective or with self-centered concerns about honor, reputation, or gain. When this kind of attitude or state happens, try to be aware that you are asleep. Once you think about your state from the Work or from something else true that you have learned and you realize that you are identifying with your negative state, then you are starting to awaken. You may even begin to feel some separation from the negative state.

The Work term "self-remembering" refers to an effort to pull yourself away from identifying with negative emotions and to lift the feeling of who you are into that observation.

If you made a clean clear break from a negative emotion and you were no longer identifying with it, then you would feel awake, and the world would look brighter. You would see clearly that IT was angry or upset, but you wouldn't feel upset or angry. You would be in a state of "self-remembering" and awake, rather than being asleep.

There are some obstacles to self-remembering. The Work tells us many things about the side of the self called "the dark side." The Work also explains how "buffers" block our awareness of our dark sides.

Before you do any Work, you think you are a fine person. You think you have a few faults, but mostly you are a decent person. After you do the Work for a while, you find out that you are not such a good person; in fact, much of the time you are anything but good. Through self-observation you find out, for example, that you often have anger or contempt toward others.

This kind of discovery throws light upon our "dark sides," the aspects of our personalities we hid from ourselves before we started doing the Work. We previously suppressed our dark side, were oblivious to it, or denied it. If we were upset or angry, we had a justifiable reason that seemed to make sense. So we continued to hide from ourselves. We were puzzled if we heard that someone didn't like us or was angry at us. How could that be? We couldn't remember doing anything to them or being objectionable in any way.

Of course, we could not remember being objectionable because we had our "buffers" to protect us or hide our dark side from ourselves. Other people see our dark side, but we don't.

Here is an example of a buffer: You are driving and come to a four-way stop. Then a woman cuts across in front of you. You start to say, "You stupid so and so . . ." when you notice that the woman is a friend of yours, a friend whose intelligence you admire and value greatly. So you wave and say, "Hello." At that point, you normally do not go back and evaluate your previous emotion of anger, nor do you recall how you felt or what you almost said. You really thought the person cutting in front of you was stupid before you realized it was your friend! You felt you were justified in your anger toward that unknown person. But when the anger fell away as you recognized your friend, as good memories and feelings came up, you immediately (that is, automatically) stopped reflecting upon the negative state that had been with you. That is the way that buffers operate.

Instead, if you are in the Work, you immediately bring that negative thought and feeling back and observe it, looking at it promptly from the light of the truth. You wake up and compare the two states. You thought the person was stupid, but you know her well enough to know that she actually is very intelligent. You felt your anger was justified, but when you knew who it was you realized you like that person.

Working shows you that the next time a similar thing happens at a four-way stop and you start to say, "You stupid . . ." you don't have to believe it. IT thinks that person cutting in front of you is stupid, but the real you might like the person if you got to know him or her.

We have so many false pictures in our minds of what we are like. We may think of ourselves as a broad-minded person who is very accepting of people. Rather, it is our friends who are so critical of everyone. We don't even connect those two ideas and see that we are criticizing our friends for being critical! Buffers are so quick that we don't even notice the inconsistencies in our own attitudes.

As we reflect upon ourselves, more and more of our buffers become apparent. By Working, we can start to get rid of those buffers.

The Work says that, before we started the Work, we thought our friends were the people who helped us. They may have helped us move, they may have come to us in times of need, listened to our stories, laughed at our jokes.

However, the Work says that the people who can really help us are those whom we do not like. We can wonder, from a Work point of view, "Why is it that I don't like those people? Why are my feelings about them so negative?"

The Work also offers a tool for exploring these kinds of questions, a tool called "external considering," and there are different ways to practice it.

One way is to observe a person you do not like and try to find a similar state within yourself. Imagine yourself in the shoes of that person and search for a time when you felt that way, looked that way, or spoke that way. If you see that person doing something that you feel you would never do, look for it in yourself. Look for something similar, a like emotion, thought, or habit, that perhaps expresses itself in a different way. Your dislike is showing you something about yourself. It is a mirror for you.

Other people who can do a lot for you are those people who dislike you. You might wonder why they dislike you. What is it about you that they find objectionable? How could it be? What is the nugget of truth within their disliking you?

Another form of external considering involves trying to experience yourself from someone else's point of view. This is far more difficult than trying to recognize another person's state within yourself. However, to vividly imagine another person's experience of you as objectionable and to see the dark side of yourself without your usual justification or rationalization are amazing experiences. Imagine what it feels like to experience *you* from your five-year-old's or your teenager's point of view or your boss's point of view. Try experiencing yourself from the viewpoint of the guy who just beeped his horn at you because you didn't start or stop fast enough.

By practicing "external considering," you can broaden your picture of who you are. And when you take the time and make the effort to Work, you will find that your negative state will become passive.

Here is a quote from the New Testament that concerns different spiritual states:

> Jesus answered, "Are there not twelve hours of daylight? Those who walk during the day do not stumble, because they see the light of this world. But those who walk at night stumble, because the light is not with them."   — John 11:9–10

The following passage from Swedenborg discusses spiritual states also, quoting what Jesus says in John 9:4:

> "Night" stands for falsity deriving from evil. "The light" stands for truth deriving from good, for just as all the light of truth derives from good, so all the night of falsity does so from evil. . . . "We must work the works of him who sent me while it is day; night is coming when no one can work."
> — *Secrets of Heaven* §2353[3, 4]

Spiritually, it is light when we see things as they are from the truth, from a Work I in our rational minds rather than from a negative I in our natural minds (IT) or from the appearance of things. When we are seeing from a spiritual point of view, we can Work! Of course, if we have a negative emotion and identify with it, then it is dark. And no matter what we try to do from that state of darkness, we will stumble.

Waking up, we begin to experience more and more states as night or day, as darkness or light, not as something theoretical and allegorical, but as an actual experience. We become more aware of those times we are thinking in darkness, when our minds are racing and the external world makes us think that this or that event made us angry or that we are justified in our negative feelings. We come to recognize when we are in the darkness.

To the degree that we observe IT noncritically and separate ourselves from IT, thus seeing the truth about the situation or state, to that degree we will feel a lightness and will gain insight, will see things from a different point of view. We become aware that we are now looking at things more from the light. It might not be a bright light; it might be like the light at dawn or even evening light, but it will be a lot lighter than pitch-dark midnight, which is pure identification with a negative state.

Being Asleep

How many of you know or have realized that you can take a typical situation, a typical event, in a different way from what you have ordinarily done?

. . . I say it is a good exercise in the morning to try to take everything that happens, all the usual discords and unpleasant tasks and so on, in an entirely new way, if you can, for a short time.[1]

---

1. Nicoll, *Commentaries*, 816–817.

When we are spiritually asleep or when IT is active, we tend to act like a puppet or respond like a machine. We respond to events automatically, without thinking, effort, or attention.

For example, if someone steps in front of me, I feel angry and resentful. That's it. I don't have to think about it; my reaction takes no effort or attention. My reaction is in my machinery. It's hardwired. I'm good at it!

Different machines react differently, but in general we are routine. In any recurring situation, there are at least ten different ways of responding, but usually we respond the same way each time, even though we get tired and bored with our own reaction.

When we watch the self, we notice how we repeat our responses. If we can begin to respond consciously, we will be able to act from a higher level of our mind rather than from the lower level of IT.

When we wake up and observe where we are, we will see a great many negative things in ourselves. Of course, the importance of not identifying with those negatives and not attributing them to ourselves has been stressed. The goal is to experience ourselves objectively, rather than subjectively—that is, not from *within* a negative thought or selfish love (subjectively) but as someone who just *has* a negative thought or selfish love (an objective experience).

What we see is true in one sense, and we have to get a picture of what is there before the Lord can help us. Only when we look at the positive side of ourselves can we be available for his help.

Here is an aphorism that might not sound so important at first; but, if you are in a negative emotion and you remember to use this quote, you will see the power and wisdom of it: "*To non-identify take nothing seriously except the Work.*"[2] The burned dinner is of no consequence. The late meeting is of no consequence. Being interrupted is of no consequence. There is

---

2. Nicoll, *Commentaries*, 812.

only one thing that is important, and that is doing the spiritual work that the Lord asks us to do:

> "Do not store up for yourselves treasures on earth, where moth and rust consume and where thieves break in and steal; but store up for yourselves treasures in heaven, where neither moth nor rust consumes and where thieves do not break in and steal."   — Matthew 6:19–20

We can live more objectively, and to do that we observe our dark sides. We can't afford to be complacent, asleep, and thinking we are doing okay spiritually when we are not. If we die before we learn how to live, do you think we can enter heaven? Imagine trying to enter heaven filled with anger or contempt for other people or irritation that other people win the lottery or have good luck! We cannot enter heaven until we separate from those kinds of states. And we do not have forever to change the kinds of states we entertain.

Redefining Failure and Success

When we start to do the Work, we begin to observe ourselves, attempt not to identify, separate from negative states, and put our sense of who we are into the observing part of ourselves.

We will not be successful in doing all these things all the time. We could define that situation as failure, but it is very important that we do not have a feeling of failure about our efforts.

Tennis instructors tell us about "inner tennis." The instructor puts a bucket down on the tennis court and tells the student to hit the ball without intending to do anything definite. The student just hits the ball in the direction of the bucket, without judgment. By doing that, the student learns faster than when he is determined to hit the ball directly into the bucket and gets angry when he misses it. Instructors claim that frustration and limited attitude prevent learning, whereas noncritical observation in sports teaches the most.

It is the same in the Work. The object is to stay awake and observe ourselves noncritically. Some of the things we observe about ourselves will be negative, or bad, because that is where we often live. We don't have to defend it, don't have to justify it, or say it is good (because it is not good); it is just that way at present.

We learn to redefine success and failure.

Suppose there are two men, both alcoholics. Neither realizes that he is alcoholic. Both are in the stage called denial. Both are good businessmen, never miss a day of work, and are still functioning in other ways.

Let's say a friend came up to both of these men and said, "Look, you guys have a problem with alcohol and should probably give it up."

They each answer, "No, I don't. I can stop drinking any time I want to."

The friend says, "Okay. I bet you one hundred dollars that neither of you can stop drinking for sixty days."

Both men take the bet.

The first man goes to the bar and drinks bitter lemon. He misses the whiskey a lot. He is somewhat surprised at how much he wants a drink, but he keeps thinking about the bet. He thinks to himself that, as soon as the sixty days are up, he can drink whatever he wants again. He thinks he can make it, and he is going to show the friend that he can stop for sixty days. And, in fact, he does avoid drinking for sixty days. He's a little shaken, but he made it.

The friend is surprised and gives him the one hundred dollars, remarking, "Good job!" Then the man immediately says to the bartender, "I want a double bourbon on the rocks, a sidecar, and a blackberry brandy. Keep them coming, and I'm buying drinks for everybody in the house." He drinks more that night than he ever drank in one night before. That man was apparently successful and thinks he had a very good sixty days.

The second man did not have such a good sixty days. He went to the bar and he too, at first, was drinking bitter lemon. He noticed that he was shaking and that started him thinking about his condition. What had he said? "I can stop drinking any time I want to!" Well, he wondered, why don't I want to? How would I go about wanting to? He started to worry about that. He noticed how much he was looking forward to the sixty days being over. He was surprised at how much he wanted a drink. And then when he picked up his glass, he would drink that soda water, but instead of using the same glass to get a refill, he would take the glass next to him from which someone else had been drinking gin. The ice cubes still had some gin on them, and he could taste it. On the way to the bathroom, he would pick up a glass that still actually had some liquid left in it. He told himself, "I'm not really drinking; I just want something cold." But he started looking for glasses that had a little more left in them; and when he went home, he started having just a quick shot or two of whiskey before bed. When his friend asked him how he was doing he said, "Oh fine, no problem. It's easier than I thought." It bothered him, however, that he was lying, and he was sneaking alcohol. He was very upset.

When the sixty days were over, the friend handed the second man the money and said, "Congratulations! I am really surprised you made it. You have more strength than I thought. Here's your one hundred dollars."

But the man handed back the money and said, "Forget it. I lost. I was a total failure. I can't stop drinking even if I want to, and I can't stop wanting it. I need some help. This has been the worst sixty days in my life!"

Well, now, who really had a bad sixty days, and who had a good sixty days? Who is closer to where he needs to be? Failure, if you look at it in those terms, is often not failure at all, but the first step toward success. The issue is not so much whether you take the drink, but what you learned. Did you learn what you needed to learn? That is success.

In terms of the Work, the alcoholic who won the hundred dollars failed. The man who did *not* win the bet was successful.

How do we know when we succeed in a spiritual trial? Consider this quote from Swedenborg:

> The trials in which we are victorious entail the belief that everyone else is more worthy than we are, and that we are more like those in hell than those in heaven, for ideas such as these present themselves to us during times of trial. After the crisis ends, then, if we enter into ways of thinking that are contrary to this outlook, it is a sign that we have not been victorious, for the thoughts we have after the struggle are capable of being turned in the direction of the thoughts we had during the struggle.   — *Secrets of Heaven* §2273[2]

Notice that the quote says nothing about doing or not doing the evil we thought about doing. Instead it discusses the kinds of thoughts we might have after the period of struggle. If we think we are great or superior to others after we've refrained from doing something bad, we did not really succeed in working through the challenge. If we had really succeeded, we'd feel humble.

The fact is that we cannot get anywhere, spiritually, without humiliation. What is humiliation? It is when we think we are pretty hot stuff and we go show off, make a fool of ourselves, and then are humiliated, humbled.

Sounds bad, right? Wrong. In the Work, unless we become humiliated, we cannot succeed. So think of failure as success!

Consider this quote from Swedenborg concerning the importance of humiliation:

> The reason a state of humility is vital to worship itself is that insofar as the heart is humbled self-love and all resulting evil come to an end; and insofar as these come to an end, good and truth, that is, charity and faith, flow in from the Lord. For above all else what stands in the way of their being received is

self-love. Indeed within self-love lies contempt for all others in comparison with ourselves; within self-love lies hatred and revenge if we are not worshipped.

— *Secrets of Heaven* §2327[3]

The state of humiliation requires what we would call "failure." Anyone who has dealt with people in addictions knows that failure is a necessary state prior to recovery. In the Work, it is a necessary state too.

So, when we observe ourselves and a negative or selfish state comes that we find we cannot fight against, just stay awake. That's vital. Eventually we will be better able to use the information we gather in order to change.

With observation, we can become aware that the good that comes through us is from the Lord. And if we have enough observation to see that, we might be able to be genuinely helpful to someone else. Being in this kind of state is like an alcoholic finally coming to say, "I cannot stay sober by myself. I am helpless. It is impossible. I need the help of a higher power." He has finally come to the point where it might be possible to recover and eventually help others. The alcoholic who is still saying, "I can quit whenever I want to" is not close to help yet. He is too full of himself.

Swedenborg wrote, "Everything bad, especially smugness, takes away a state of peace" (*Secrets of Heaven* §8455[2]). If we are confident in the Lord, we can be peaceful. But if we place all our confidence in self, we cannot be peaceful because we cannot really trust what is from self. Our confidence then is like a house built on sand, and it is not going to stand when the storm comes. If our confidence is in the Lord, it cannot be shaken, for we can be—and are—confident that whatever happens contributes to our spiritual welfare. In that state, we have no sense of success or failure. We will not depend on things going our way but the Lord's way.

✹

The Task for Chapter 2

Begin by writing down the typical ways you react in three different situations.

For instance, one of my typical reactions is to get irritated when my wife suggests an activity for the evening. If my wife says, "Let's go to the movies," I get irritated. If she says, "I don't want to go to the movies," I get irritated. If she says, "We are having company tonight," I get irritated. If she tells me, "They can't come over tonight," I may get irritated. IT is just irritated. The first answer out of IT's mouth is, "No." It is ridiculous.

However, when my wife says, "Let's have someone over for dinner," I'm saying "No," but my daughter says, "Great!" So, I can see from my daughter's reaction that there is another way to take my wife's suggestion that is not my usual way. (I try not to take myself too seriously, and, fortunately, my wife doesn't take me too seriously either. If we did take me seriously, we might just live alone somewhere in the woods.)

List your typical ways of taking things or reacting in three different situations, and then list a different way of responding to each situation. For example, you might begin by writing down these typical responses: #1 irritated (in Situation A), #2 jealous (in Situation B), and #3 anxious (in Situation C). Then write down a different way that you could respond to each situation. If you want to make them *better* ways, fine, but you don't have to; just list three ways you could react differently from your normal reaction.

CHAPTER 3
Our Effects on Others

All evil is contagious.
— *Emanuel Swedenborg*

Often when I am talking about the Work and I use religious terms, some people get uncomfortable. If I start talking about "evil" or "good," or mention heaven and hell, some people may have a negative reaction due to their prior associations with those words. But the more I do and read about the Work the more I realize that religion is not something we can separate from our lives, even if some of our prior experiences with religion have been unsatisfying. I also realize more and more that religious terms can be very practical.

Because they have different religious backgrounds, some people may think of some words or terms as religious, while other people do not. An example is the word *falsity*. Of course, there are a number of terms most everyone connects with religion, terms like *heaven*, *hell*, and the *Ten Commandments*.

Here are ways we can think of some basic terms in practical, religious ways:

- *Heaven*   When you are happy and at peace, when you have good communication and feel close to someone, when you are feeling warm toward someone, these times are like heaven! It feels like the kingdom of God is within you.

- *Hell*   When you are in an angry, bitter mood, fighting with your friend, your spouse, or your children, you are in hell. You are cold and shut down.
- *Falsehood* When you believe something that is untrue. Suppose something is wrong with your car, and you think it was the carburetor, although that's not really the problem. Your thought about the carburetor is a falsehood.
- *Evil*   When something prevents you (or others) from doing good or pulls you (or others) toward hell. Let's say that you brought your car to a mechanic and told him that the carburetor is on the blink. Instead of fixing the real problem, he "fixes" your carburetor and charges you for that. The mechanic has done something evil.
- *Truth*   When a piece of information or a fact can help bring about good in your life. Continuing with our car example, if indeed your original thought that the carburetor is the problem is correct, then that truth could contribute to a good result—the carburetor could be fixed, and the car would run fine.
- *Good*   When you (or others) are drawn closer to heaven and take pleasure in the experience. If you know the truth, have the tools, and Work, then you can bring about good. You might think, "What's so good about a car starting?" It's not just the car starting; it's what you can do with a car and how you feel about it. You can take your children to school, you can pick up the groceries, you can go on a vacation, and enjoy doing those things.

Just as, in the previous chapter, we discussed redefining the terms *success* and *failure*, we often have to readjust our views about religious or moral concepts. Another example is the idea of the Ten Commandments.

We often think of the Ten Commandments as rules to make us behave, but we might instead consider them to be directions the Lord gives us so that we can receive the wonderful states he wants us to enjoy. The Lord created us so that he could share what is good, or heaven, with us. The Lord doesn't say, "Thou shalt not commit adultery" just to be mean-spirited. He says this because he wants to give us the joys in our marriage that he can't give us if we are committing adultery. With the Ten Commandments, the Lord is trying to lead us to heaven, not just give us rules.

Erasing the Oppositional Perspective

We have stressed the importance of working on yourself as the first step in spiritual renewal. You might think that doing this Work will make you self-centered, but the opposite is true. The Work has you observe yourself and examine your negative states, and the more you do this the less self-centered you will become. So, observing yourself can lessen the barriers you put between yourself and other people.

Other Work tools can produce a similar effect. Chapter 2 introduced the Work tool called "external considering." One way to use this tool is to try to imagine yourself actually being another person, especially someone you find objectionable. Imagine yourself in their body and try to get in touch with their posture and how they feel physically. Then try to get in touch with what this other person thinks.

An actor may be given the role of playing a pompous king, although he himself is a humble person. In order to play the part, the actor would have to step into a king's body, taking the posture of the king, then trying to think like a king and feel like a king. When he could totally, as it were, become that embodiment, the audience would believe in him as the king. That is like external considering.

The more fully you can use external considering, the more impact it will have, especially in producing a more balanced effect in your life. Using this tool will begin to erase the oppositional perspective, the "me-versus-them" viewpoint. The division between you and others will fade somewhat because you will be able to more fully experience other people.

But sometimes you might not want to try to experience another person, especially when you feel that doing so will bring on a negative state in you. Such might be the case if the other person is behaving in an evil manner, and you are afraid to imagine yourself as that person. Should you try external considering anyway? Yes! To see why, you must recognize several related facts.

First, the Lord directs us to love our enemy and bless those who curse us. External considering is a way of showing love for someone toward whom we are reacting negatively (with excessive fear, anger, or contempt).

Second, there is no such thing as one isolated emotion. For example, we have a word for anger, but that word is just a description of the experience, although anger is not just one isolated, negative state. If you really observe anger, you will find that it does not stay the same. The intensity changes, the feeling comes and goes, and also there are related emotions such as impatience, irritation, or frustration. Emotions or negative states associate with each other, and sometimes they infect each other, you might say. Still, it is possible for emotions to change greatly, from positive to negative or from negative to positive. External considering can help you notice how your emotions are changing.

Third, despite appearances to the contrary, we create our own spiritual environments within ourselves. Suppose we come in contact with someone we dislike and we become upset. The fact is that the other person does not cause, but only activates, our own negativity.

Ray Silverman, Swedenborgian minister, studied passages in Swedenborg's writings concerning the contagion of negativity. He initially studied passages concerning being careful with whom you associate, since evils are contagious. At first, Silverman thought that certain people themselves might be contagious, but then he came to realize that Swedenborg might be referring to *states* within us that relate to who we are and where we are spiritually:

> At first I took [Swedenborg's assertion that all evils are conta-
> gious, in *True Christianity* §120] quite literally and understood
> it to mean that I should be extremely wary of the people I asso-
> ciated with. The passage is quite strong, stating that "whoev-
> er associates with robbers or pirates at length becomes like
> them, . . . for all evils are contagious and they might be
> compared to the plague, which is communicated merely by the
> breath of emanation from the infected." . . .
>
> Gradually I came to see how very useful this teaching is,
> especially for young people. . . . However, I also saw that these
> words had deeper and broader implications. This happened
> when I began to see them beyond the confines of physical time
> and space. I began to see them as words that did not so much dic-
> tate who my acquaintances in this world should be, but rather
> what thoughts I should entertain. These words began to speak
> to me not so much about my physical surroundings and associ-
> ates, but about my spiritual environment-the thoughts and
> feelings I invited into my mind, associated with, and embraced.
> . . . This was the "new light" in which I *now* saw those words,
> "All evils are contagious."[1]

With regard to another person, our initial reaction may be
anger. This reaction activates our lower or negative self. And
once active, IT will take over not only our activities but also
how we perceive everything and everybody. The lower self will
not be satisfied with negative feelings towards one person; IT
will soon seek out your family and loved ones. Like physical
contagion, negative emotions have a way of spreading rapidly.
IT will create an entirely negative environment for you, all
beginning with one specific, negative emotion!

So because we create our own spiritual environments and
because external considering shows us how our emotions can
change and because external considering is one way to love

---

1. Ray Silverman, "Constancy and Change in the New Church," *New Church Life*
CVIII, no. 11 (November 1988): 468. Reprinted by permission.

another person, external considering can show us that we can be free of our own negativity. When we react negatively to another person, it appears that their actions are causing our reactions. To be free of the bondage of our own negativity, we must break out of this appearance and see that the cause of the negativity is in us. If we expel this kind of negativity from our hearts (with external considering), then we receive the Lord's blessing of freedom. We will be aware that we have a choice about whether we feel negative or positive.

I mentioned earlier that Swedenborg interpreted some situations in the Bible as describing our own spiritual states. Consider Jesus' parable about the pharisee and the tax collector:

> "Two men went up to the temple to pray, one a Pharisee and the other a tax collector. The Pharisee, standing by himself, was praying thus, 'God, I thank you that I am not like other people: thieves, rogues, adulterers, or even like this tax collector. I fast twice a week; I give a tenth of all my income.' But the tax collector, standing far off, would not even look up to heaven, but was beating his breast and saying, 'God be merciful to me, a sinner!' I tell you, this man went down to his home justified rather than the other; for all who exalt themselves will be humbled, but all who humble themselves will be exalted."
>
> —Luke 18: 10–14

We can think of the pharisee's approach as describing how we act when we see only the light sides of ourselves but not our dark sides. In contrast, the tax collector calls himself a sinner and prays for forgiveness. The tax collector's approach is akin to our doing the Work and seeing clearly that we all have the negative traits we see in other people. Then we see that we are like anybody else, and, humbled, we say, "Help me, Lord."

That humility is an important step. If we don't come to that stage, we can't be justified by God. Instead, we justify ourselves.

In the past, when I used to think about this parable, I would feel a separation, a superiority, regarding the pharisee who prays in the wrong way. Now, however, I think of this story as speaking about the pharisee *within* me, and immediately my feeling of superiority dissipates.

The pharisee within constantly uses the Bible to judge and blame and condemn other people. So in the Work and from a Work point of view, watch out for your pharisee! Take on that burden, the part of you that is irritated and critical of everyone else and wants to use your Work to judge other people, just as the pharisees used the Word (the Bible) to condemn other people's behavior. As Maurice Nicoll has written, "Your best 'I's' are uncritical 'I's,' 'I's' that never judge either you or other people."[2] By not judging someone, you must not attribute people's negative states to them, anymore than you attribute your state to yourself.

Now that does not mean that you don't recognize that some of their states are negative or even disorderly or evil. But it is a mistake to believe that a negative state is the person. The state is just present with them and active at that time. Only the Lord can tell what is actually within their power to resist. So you don't attribute an evil to another person any more than you attribute states to yourself. Perhaps you have heard that we should "condemn the behavior, not the person." The Work actually requires that you live that idea.

So you can love a person and yet see that their state is disorderly. However, this attitude does not come automatically; it takes effort and attention to do that for yourself and for others.

When you reach the realization that your states are not you, then it becomes possible to do the same for other people. It becomes easier to see that people are not their state, they are just temporarily caught up in a state. You can often see this most clearly with children who may be furious and say to a

---

2. Nicoll, *Commentaries*, 817.

parent, "I hate you," but then an hour later when the state is gone, they may say, "Oh Mommy, I love you." In this way, we adults are just big children.

Living from Truth Rather Than False Ways of Thinking

We need to ask ourselves during a negative state, "How are negative thought processes justifying their existence in me at this moment? What is the false way of thinking that is convincing me to hang on to these negatives?" Unless you can identify the particular untrue thought involved, the negativity will stay with you and will make life hell for you.

To identify these falsities, we need to keep in mind the difference between the external world and the internal world. The external world is the outer, material world and whatever happens there. The internal world is our spiritual life.

We also need to be aware of the direction in which cause and effect flow. Even though the appearance is the opposite, the external world cannot enter or influence the internal world (because nothing gross can go into something fine). However, the internal world can flow out into the external world. The outside world cannot make you angry or upset, but anger or upset can come from within and justify its existence with events or conditions in the external world.

We sometimes think to ourselves, "If I only had money, I would be happy." But that is a falsity. To the degree we believe the falsity—that both the problem and solution are *out there*— to that degree negativity can exist in us. This is what the Work is about: looking within ourselves to see what kinds of internal states we let run our lives at each given moment.

The opposite of what is false is something that is true. In general, if something is true, it is good or a form of good. However, there is a kind of truth that has no good in it yet, a truth that is still just "knowledge." Knowledge is neither good nor bad. We can think of these kinds of truths or knowledge as tools we can use. For example, if your car were broken, to fix

it, you would need to know which tools would be the right
ones to fix it. A more spiritual example of a knowledge is
having an awareness of a Work tool such as "stop thought"
or external considering.

There is also another kind of truth, a truth that joins with
good. This kind of truth is "understanding," and it can exist
only when knowledge is actually used. For example, if your car
is broken, and there are tools available for you to work with,
your tools could not produce a good result (the running car)
without your effort being involved. A more spiritual illustration
of understanding is taking a Work tool such as external
considering and actually using it to gain a better appreciation
of someone else.

When we combine our knowledge of religious truths with
our use of the tools described in the Work, we begin to have
insights (understanding) that help us change for the better.
During the process of awakening, we suddenly see that IT is
evil. Our ability to recognize evil comes from divine revelation,
that is, from the truth that allows us to see clearly, to see a
state for what it is. Truth enables us to know we are looking at
evil when we observe a negative state. And as we use effort
and attention to avoid identifying with or expressing a
negative and withdraw from it, that truth starts to reveal
certain things about that evil and our own nature.

Toward what goodness are such insights trying to lead us?
The answer lies in the side or state that is opposed to the
negative. As our understanding grows and we start to put truth
to use in our lives, positive states come alive and become real.
We come to see the "goodness" within the truth.

When the Lord says he makes everything new (Revelation
21:5), try to see how that could be. He continues to make
things new, and we can go on learning to eternity.

Remember the story of Sodom and Gomorrah? In Genesis
19:17, angels tell Lot to flee, with his family, from the city of
Sodom:

> When they had brought them outside, they said, "Flee for your life; do not look back or stop anywhere in the Plain; flee to the hills, or else you will be consumed."

After Lot's escape to the town of Zoar, the Lord destroyed the cities of Sodom and Gomorrah, and he also destroyed the plain. Lot's wife looked back and was turned into a pillar of salt (Genesis 19:26). Lot and his daughters soon left Zoar and went to the mountains (Genesis 19:30).

Initially, I thought this story was instructing us not to look back at our evil states, but now I don't think that at all. The command "Do not look back," I now realize, is a command not to remain in religious teachings. That sounds strange because religious teachings are very important. But consider the following passage from Swedenborg:

> "Do not look back behind you" means that he was not to look to matters of doctrine. "And do not halt in all the plain" means that he was not to linger over any one of these. "Escape into the mountain" means towards the good that flows from love and charity. . . . For "a city" means doctrinal teaching, . . . while "a mountain" means love and charity.
> — *Secrets of Heaven* §§2424, 2417

Truth *is* an important beginning step. The story of Sodom and Gomorrah does not say not to go into the plains, since you have to go into the plains (that is, you need religious truths) to get to the mountain (a state where you can live a good life). The story says not to look back or *remain* in the plains. Instead, we should flee to the hills: we should strive for states where we can have love for one another and for the Lord.

This story illustrates the degree of effort involved in growing spiritually by actually using religious truths or knowledge, as opposed to just thinking about them. The plain is easy to get to; you just walk. To flee to the hills takes effort. You have to climb to go to the hills.

If we continue to just *think* about the truth, just talk about the truth, just read and learn about it, but when an active evil state comes to us, we don't do anything to apply the truth, then we are remaining in religious teachings. The truth alone is empty. Lot's wife turned to salt when she looked back.

It takes effort and attention to *live* the truth. This effort and attention expands our capacity to do good. In fact, it is our effort to live the truth—no matter how often we stumble and fall—that determines who we really are.

The command to "flee to the hills" is what the Work is all about, and it is why we have tasks. The important thing is what we *do* during an active negative state, not just when we are reading and contemplating religious books or listening to a sermon in church. The Lord is closer to us in temptations than at any other time, and temptations occur whenever a negative state is active.

Help in Our Struggle to Overcome Negativity

As we Work, we may feel that we are fighting a losing battle, that we have too many flaws to overcome. Just as we should redefine restrictive religious terms, we also need to rethink who is in control of our lives. We feel this thing called "life" *as if* it is our own. It appears as if we are living our lives, making our choices, having our reactions. But it only appears that way. Start observing how you actually make choices, and you may discover that you know less about that than you do about your car!

This statement has a couple of implications. The first implication is this: the Lord is fighting for us. *This is not our life; it is the Lord's life.* The actual life in our body is the Lord's life. He is the only life.

You might have the feeling when you are in temptation that the Lord doesn't know how you feel or what it is like or how hard it is. Well, it is the Lord who is fighting for you; it is not you fighting. He's fighting, and you are having the experience *as if* you were fighting. So the Lord is undergoing that temptation for you, and he couldn't be closer to you. It is his temptation as to effort, although you have the experience as if it were yours.

The other implication raises this question: If you are going through a temptation and in your own eyes you fail, whether by having a drink or getting angry when you said you wouldn't, since the Lord was doing the fighting for you, did the Lord fail? No. The Lord does not fail. If the Lord did not fail, then you did not fail. This means that failure does not lie in whether or not you took the drink or were angry, but in whether you were awake or asleep when it happened. Did you successfully get the information that the Lord wished to give you by means of the experience? That is what is important. If he chooses to give you the experience and you stay awake and get the message that he wishes to give you, then you succeed.

Try to look at your life and see that the Lord is fighting for you. Examine the implication of this in your own experience when you have a feeling of failure. Right then, during that feeling of failure, ask yourself, "What is the implication of the Lord's now being closer to me than ever, during this temptation? What does it mean that he is fighting for me?"

We can consider negative and positive attitudes even further. A negative attitude says, "I failed. I am not important. I should have done better. The Lord isn't with me." A positive attitude says, "The Lord is with me, and he never allows anything to happen unless it will be for my eternal spiritual welfare. He takes everything and turns it to what is best within whatever the experience happens to be."

Having a positive attitude is one way of trusting the Lord. You do not trust the Lord when you think that if you had just prayed harder it would have kept you from an evil. You *do* trust the Lord when you observe yourself struggling with a temptation and think that the Lord is right there with you and that he can still teach you right there within, and even by means of, that very experience.

So if you struggle with a temptation and end up giving in, don't think that the Lord deserted you and that you failed. He doesn't fail. He gives you experiences that we sometimes see as failure.

Swedenborg explains how the Lord is always with us:

> All of us, no matter how large our numbers, are withheld from evil by the Lord, and . . . this is done with a mightier power than anyone can possibly believe. For we are all perpetually bent on evil both on account of the heredity we are born with and on account of what we have acquired through our own actions, so much so that, if we were not being withheld by the Lord, we would spend every moment rushing headlong into the lowest hell. So great is the Lord's mercy, however, that we are being raised up every moment, even every fraction of a moment, and kept from rushing into that place. . . . Thus the Lord battles with us constantly, and with hell on our behalf, though it does not seem that way to us.
>
> — *Secrets of Heaven* §2406[2]

The Task for Chapter 3

The task is different from earlier tasks. Previously we observed what our habitual responses are to what other people do or say, and even what our internal responses are, our thoughts and our feelings. We do not blame anybody else for our responses. Our responses are our responses, but we do find we have to work on them.

However, in this next task we are going to focus on how other people might respond to what we do. You may say that is their problem, they should be in the Work, and they should be working on their own response. But you would be mistaken. In the Work, you get to do all the Work, and nobody else has to do anything! That is just the way Work is. Whoever wishes to be the most will be the least and vice versa.

Your task is simply to observe or guess, when a negative state is with you, before you speak or do anything to another person, what impact your remark or actions or behavior will have, or might have, on that person's state. For instance, if my child comes home ten minutes late gushing about the wonderful time she has had sliding in mud, which is obvious from the mud on her clothes and now on the carpet, I might say crossly, "You're late" or "You should have called!" If I decide to say that, I can anticipate that my child's face will fall, and my state will also descend. I can imagine my behavior will alter her reaction or response to me.

I can imagine another scenario. Let's say that I come home and my son has not done something he promised to do. When I notice this, I am annoyed, but he is walking around the house humming and happy. Now is my opportunity to mention it. Well, if I do, how do you suppose it will impact him?

You may choose to say or do the thing and observe the impact on the person's state, whether it is what you expected or whether it turns out to be stronger or weaker than you expected. On the other hand, if you choose not to say or do the thing, then use your observing energy to watch what is going on in you.

This is sort of a "spiritual theft" task. We so often steal good states away from others. We warn the honeymooners, "Just wait!" Or when a student is young and feeling good about school, someone will say, "Boy, when you get into college, things will change!"

The good news is that we can have a positive impact on people. We can consciously choose to act well. We do it with our friends. We try to have a good effect. So, "cease to do evil, learn to do good" (Isaiah 1:16–17). In the Work, we focus on our reactions and cleanse ourselves so that we can do good. The ultimate goal, of course, is to allow the Lord's influence to flow through us to other people and do *real* good to them.

CHAPTER 4
Working on Different Kinds of Negatives

Everything reveals if we are patient with it.
— *Wilson Van Dusen*

Recurring Negatives

Let's imagine you meet a woman toward whom you have a negative reaction. You know from the Work that a negative reaction is not a good thing to entertain, so whenever you see her, although your negative reaction comes up, you try to dismiss it, try to turn your attention elsewhere, try to become passive to your reaction and ignore it. Then you see the woman again and the negative reaction returns, and you go through your Work again.

It bothers you that every time you see her the same negative reaction comes up. First the negative reaction was the problem, but in time the problem becomes its recurrence. You think, "Maybe something really is wrong with that person." But your Work memory says, "No, this is not the case." So you decide to try external considering. You bring to mind the good things you know about her, but still, having heard some bad rumors, you notice that your pattern continues.

You decide to spend an hour or two with the woman and really get to know her. You ask about her life and thoughts and feelings and other things, no matter how embarrassing or ridiculous, even about the rumors you have heard. You hear all the good and the bad. After this meeting, you have a feeling of completion. You have a clear picture or idea of who this person is. Most important of all is that you feel you know her and understand who she really is.

Then the next time you see this person, you don't have the old negative reaction. You have a good open feeling.

In my job as a probation officer, I made pre-sentence reports about people who committed crimes. The U.S. attorney would tell me what bad thing the man had done. But then I would talk to his wife, and she would tell me he is a wonderful guy, good to the children and so forth. As I was doing my investigation, I would go back and forth in regard to how I felt about my client. Then finally I would sit down with the real person and ask him every question I could think of, to really get to know him.

Once I interviewed a man who had ordered child pornography. When I was new in law enforcement, I would have asked him general questions because I would have been too embarrassed to ask him detailed ones. I would try to make my decision based on a general impression. But after having been in the business for many years, I would ask every possible question. My client might start shaking and get very embarrassed, but I did not get embarrassed. I could make my decision based on all the information I needed or wanted, knowing there was no relevant question about this person that I had failed to ask.

Sometimes it is very useful to take a recurring negative emotion and the internal monologue that accompanies it and just let it say everything it wants to say. If you can arrange for a partner or friend to be there to listen to you, this exercise can be even more useful than doing it alone, because you are apt to better hear what you are saying when someone else is listening. Just take the recurring negative emotion and speak from that emotion for as long as you can. Don't think about it, and don't edit it. Just keep talking until that feeling has said *everything* it has to say.

This is a surprisingly difficult exercise to do. It is hard to keep it going. It is like interrogating a criminal; once you address a negative directly and start asking questions, the negative doesn't want to talk anymore because you are learning things about it!

Some of what your negative emotion will say will be ridiculous, but just let it come out. However, this has to be an objective effort. Don't let yourself get distracted and dwell on statements like, "This is silly, I don't want to say this."

If a friend of yours says he is having a difficult time in his marriage, you might say, "Tell me about it." If he said, "I don't think my wife really loves me," you wouldn't say, "Oh, that's silly! Of course she cares for you! Don't talk like that!" You would see that it is better just to let him talk about the situation for a while and let his true feelings and thoughts surface. He might say, "She doesn't even seem to like me." If you ask him to tell you more, he might say, "It makes me really sad. I'm scared and nervous that she might leave me." You encourage him to keep talking, until he gets it all out.

When you do this exercise, just say what you have to say, and you will find from doing it that a lot of things will come up, and you will get to see them with more clarity.

Working on a recurring negative without the needed scrutiny is like Working either because someone else said you should or because somehow you believe that anything negative has to be shoved away immediately, without being closely examined. If a negative recurs even when you Work on it, then the particulars of that negative are not clear enough, and you need to empty it all out to look at whatever is false about it.

Recurring negatives are linked with our memories. And there are many false beliefs within our memories. One reason is that we remember from our "level of being" at the time the event occurred. So a three-year-old given a small toy when he was looking for a big toy on Christmas may have a memory of a mean mother or a stingy father. He has no memory of twelve brothers and sisters also receiving small toys and a father who was unemployed. He is only remembering from the small point of his level of being at that age of three years, so that memory is not an objective one. We have to begin to see that bad memories have false elements in them. What bad memories claim is not really true even though they look true and sound true.

Once you can listen to a recurring negative with more clarity, separation can take place. Separation is the whole point of the emptying-out process. If you cut examination off too fast, the negative emotion will return.

The Observing I in this tell-it-all process is key. The Observing I is the person listening to you, or your intention to do the exercise in order to learn more about the negative.

Once you know specifically what within a negative attitude is false and where that leads, then the next time the negative comes up, you can choose to drop it because of what you have seen. You will not be dropping the negative because of historical faith (a faith based on tradition or the beliefs of others) or a general effort to do the Work. You will drop the negative because you understand the false concept within it and because you yourself have decided to let it go.

Entangled Negatives

Jesus told a parable about the wheat and the tares (or weeds):

> "The kingdom of heaven may be compared to someone who sowed good seed in his field; but while everybody was asleep, an enemy came and sowed weeds among the wheat, and then went away. So when the plants came up and bore grain, then the weeds appeared as well."   —Matthew 13:24–26

His servants asked whether they should pull up the tares, and the man replied:

"Let both of them grow together until the harvest; at the
harvest time I will tell the reapers, Collect the weeds first and
bind them in bundles to be burned, but gather the wheat into
my barn."   — Matthew 13:30

Sometimes, when we are doing our tasks, we can find
legitimate pain mixed with self-pity, anger, or other negative
emotions. This is because some negatives, such as self-pity, can
have dual causes that involve legitimate past hurt. Here's an
example. A little child wants to help dust the living room but
accidentally breaks a vase and receives a severe scolding from
her mother. The child's motive is good, but the experience
would result in mixed emotions and a false message. As an
adult, she may get easily upset if a glass is broken and may
wonder why such a small thing bothers her. By letting the I
that gets easily upset have its complete say, she might come to
understand her recurring negative when small accidents
happen.

It is important to get things in clear view and to make a
separation between good intentions and motives that have
been injured and negatives that need Work, even though the
good motives and the negatives may seem to have similar
reactions to the one event.

Swedenborg wrote about separation:

> All who enter the next life are taken back to a life similar to that
> which they were leading during their lifetime. Then in the case
> of the good, evil and falsity are separated so that the Lord may
> raise these people up by means of good and truth into heaven;
> but in the case of the evil, good and truth are separated so that
> those evil ones may be carried away by means of evil and falsity
> into hell, . . . in exact accord with the Lord's words in
> Matthew, "To those who have, it will be given, so that they
> may have more abundantly; but from those who have not, even
> what they have will be taken away" (Matthew 13:12). And
> elsewhere in the gospel, "To all those who have, it will be

given, so that they may have in abundance; but from those who have not, it will be taken away" (Matt. 25:29). The same is meant by the following words which appear in Matthew, "Let both grow together until the harvest; and at the time of harvest I will tell the reapers, 'Gather the weeds first and bind them in bundles to burn them, but gather the wheat into my barn.'" (Matt. 13:30). The same point is made in the description of the net thrown into the sea, gathering fish of various kinds, and how after that the good were sorted into vessels while the bad were thrown away (Matt. 13:47–50). . . . *For in the next life, such is the communication of all ideas comprising thought, and of all affections, that goodness is communicated to the good, and evil to the evil. . . . Consequently unless separation took place, countless harmful things would result.*
— *Secrets of Heaven* §2449[2, 3], (emphasis added)

The separation process first requires observation. We need to get thoughts and emotions out in the open, see the particulars of them, and hear them; then we can start separating the good feelings from the bad feelings.

Hazy Negatives

Imagine a circle within which are represented by dots all possible states of mind. In the circle is a lot of little black dots and some big black dots. All the black dots represent negative states.

We could say that the big black dots represent those states we *recognize* as our negative states, the ones we know the Lord wants us to work on. There is no question about these kinds of states. An example is hate. I know the Lord doesn't want me to hate anyone; so if I feel hatred, I know, for sure, it is a negative state. Another might be contempt. I know contempt isn't good. Some people struggle about whether or not anger is beneficial, so that may be an open question for some of you. Still, there are states within ourselves we easily recognize as negative—states that are selfish or harmful to ourselves or others.

There are other states that are not as clear. Let's say that some of the little black dots are clustered together in places; these represent problem areas. For example, you may admit to having a high stress level in your life but find it hard to see this as an object of Work. A person can be in denial about stress as much as he can be in denial about alcohol or drugs. A person might say, "Well, I have stress, but it is no big problem. I get to work every day. I handle my family life okay, and although there is some stress at home and I sometimes need to take an antacid to ease my stomach or a shot of whiskey to calm down, it's no big problem." If you listen to someone talking like that, you will be reminded of an alcoholic talking. The talk has the same content as an alcoholic's who thinks of himself as just a social drinker. Drinking hasn't caused enough of a problem yet for the alcoholic to see it clearly. You hear the denial. The reality is still on that person's dark side. We know he is an alcoholic, but he hasn't come to that recognition yet. People have to come to see negative realities for themselves. But before they can be clearly seen, certain negatives can appear very hazy.

We want to make our own hazy areas of negativity clear. We want to understand that those hazy areas are not isolated small problems; they are related, like the small black dots that start to cluster. If the drinker who does not recognize his problem talked to a counselor the counselor might ask, "How much money do you spend on alcohol?" The client starts to realize what his habit costs. "How does alcohol affect you?" "Well, I just relax for the evening. If my children come in, I may yell at them and make them let me alone so I can relax." The drinker begins to see that yelling isn't so good and that it may be connected to his drinking. In my own case years ago, when I told someone I only had three drinks a day, he asked how much time I spent thinking about those three drinks. "Well, all the time," I had to admit. I would always be asking myself,

"Am I going to have one at lunch and two for supper? Or should I have all three after supper?" I thought about drinking all day.

The amount of time we spend thinking about something is very telling. The amount of time we spend in a state of worry, tension, or anxiety may be a bigger problem than we consider it to be. If you observe how much time you are giving to a state, you may see that it is a real problem. Things that pop up at three o'clock and again at six o'clock are related, and they impact your family, your job, every aspect of your life. They are definitely a problem.

Prevailing Negatives

We can also consider how some states occur as an on-going prevailing negativity that just settles in and stays in readiness, exploding whenever it receives a pinprick. Think about what happens to a balloon that has been blown up as much as it can be but then is given one more puff of air. BAM! It will burst. Many of us live constantly at that degree of intensity, and when something extra comes along, we just explode.

Being tense is so constant with me that it just feels normal. That is like an alcoholic who needs to take two drinks to feel normal. My normal state seems to be a tense, worried, hurried feeling. If I stop and relax, it feels so unusual I don't know what to do with it! I want to rush back to being hurried and worried because that is my norm. So, I want to focus on that anxious state so I can see how to dissolve the related negative states. It will take what the Work calls "long observation" just to look at them. Maybe I will have to talk to someone, one on one. The person I talk to might ask, "What is it that you get nervous about?" I might answer, "Well, about giving classes." Then I can get into the particulars rather than be in the general negative and aware only that I am nervous. Once I can see that IT is nervous, I can apply the Work. If I don't Work, this state of anxiety can eat up my life. I can spend my whole life being anxious!

I want to see how such negative states go about spending an entire day with me. I want to get very clear on that, with particulars. If I wanted to build a house I wouldn't want to know in general what it would look like, I would want to know specifically. I want to know specifically about this state in me, so that I can apply the Work to it.

You may have heard the phrase "perpetual unrest." The state of perpetual unrest comes from selfish loves. In contrast, the Lord says things like these: *Be still and know that I am God* (Psalms 46:10), and *Let the whole earth keep silence before him* (Habakkuk 2:20), and *Come to me all you that are weary and are carrying heavy burdens, and I will give you rest* (Matthew 11:28). The Lord speaks of peace beyond all telling and of being like a little child, innocent and joyful.

When I compare my own usual state to these quotes, I realize it is a sin to spend my life in a low level of anxiety, when the Lord really wants me to have trust, confidence, peace, and joy. I have touches of those peaceful, trusting states, but I want to spend more time there. In fact, I want to live there, in those states God promises are possible.

Flashes of the Future

I observe that states of negativity, as they pop up, provide quick pictures of the possible future. They are hazy quick flashes of what could happen in half an hour, or later in the day, or sometime in the future. For me, these pictures are almost always from associations of fear, anxiety, or some worry that might concern me. If I'm going to go visit someone's house I'll think, "I'm going to wake her up, and she won't be happy." Or, if I have to go to court for my job, I'll think, "What if I don't know the answer to the questions I'm asked?" Hazy messages tell me that whatever the situation, it is going to be bad. I am aware of the flash, and I try to cut it off as soon as I can and try to relax. I try to feel what trust would be like, try to feel the difference and notice the distinction. Then, when I actually experience the real situation, what happens is not anything like what the flash predicted!

There was one time in my job as a probation officer when I had to tell a man that he owed my office money. I had flashes beforehand of what would occur: it was near Thanksgiving, and I thought it would be embarrassing for the man to say he could not pay the money. All day little flashes came to me of how awkward it would be. Then, I went to his house, and the sky was blue, and the man wasn't home. I left a note and that was that; my actual experience was nothing like the flash picture!

It is important to be aware of positive flashes of the future as well as negative ones because a positive picture can be a set-up. Suppose you have positive flashes of your upcoming vacation. Your experience isn't really going to turn out exactly as you imagine it, of course, even though you may come to depend upon it. If reality turns out differently from what we expect, it can spoil our experience. In time, you can learn to sense those I's that are just a set-up and can stop them before they get force. As long as you know that the advance picture is not reality, you can use the picture. But if you have expectations that cannot adapt to whatever happens, then you are liable to have a negative experience. You might even lose all the benefit of being on vacation.

We have to turn toward, or trust, the Lord, in order to fight a negative state. How do we actually do that at the moment a negative state is upon us? One way I have found to work is to relax the body and then call on things I know from the Lord. I can say to myself, "Let the Lord handle it. I'll do what I can and everything will be okay."

If part of us doesn't want to believe everything will be okay and that the Lord is present, we can ask simply, "How would I act if I did believe it?" We may still often be in the middle of negative states, but we can Work on them and get more clarity about them each time.

When you are Working, if you trust the Lord in the little details, he will use the process for your eternal spiritual welfare.

If you can have the necessary trust, then the higher part of you is trusting even while the lower natural mind may be riddled with fears. Try to put the feeling of *who you are* into the trust part of yourself instead of the fear-filled part. Remember, the part of you that thinks any situation has to "be different," the part of you that thinks, "I have to do something to change this state, or make this state go away" (instead of just observing the negative state), that part of you is trusting in *yourself*, not in the Lord. Whose opinion is it that the state should go away at once? The Lord is in charge of the most minute things, so every situation is the way it should be, at the moment, for your eternal spiritual welfare. He will use that state. Just accept the state you are in, and the Lord will change it when he is ready. Acceptance of what is, even though IT doesn't accept it, is a necessary step that the Lord allows within his providence.

Often in retrospect, looking back on terrible states, I realize I received something from going through the terrible state that I might never have gotten from what I might call an elevated state.

When we start to separate from a negative state, part of our awareness can rise up into the rational mind, and then we can look down on the negative state. The negative state is still there, but we will be above it for the time being.

The Work is the only important thing, a turning toward the Lord. We can feel that, and it is a spiritual experience. Perhaps we have felt it in overcoming some big black negative states. So we can believe that it is possible to change in regard to smaller negatives that may have become a generalized anxiety in us.

If you were a body builder, you would know a person can't change physically without effort and attention. You can't build muscles without using effort and attention. It is not quite as clear that it takes effort and attention to relax. You might think that to relax you just have to do nothing; but if you do nothing, you may have a general state of anxiety, worry, and stress. It can take as much effort to become contented as it does to come to any other new state. The Lord promises us a lot, but we still have to exert effort to make it happen.

Author Wilson Van Dusen describes another way of experiencing life rather than from worldly cares and anxieties. We are not just out here in the desert. There is a promised land:

> Everything reveals if we are patient with it.
> . . . In the mystical mood I allow all there is to speak, to affect me. . . .
> It is the practice of openness to what is here. Like the aesthetic person, the mystic is in an appreciation of things as they are. This moment is perfect. It is all here, all there is.
> There is a tremendous nowness to the mystical experience. It is as though all there ever was passes through this present into all there ever will be. One rests in such a moment. Questions have no place. Doubts are absent. . . .
> The experience is up through the core of one's being. Words are not necessary.[1]

In Chapter 3 we saw that the biblical advice not to remain in the plain, but to flee to the hills instead, means that we should not remain in doctrine but instead seek a life of love or charity.

We can "flee to the hills" by avoiding evils or withdrawing from them. However, as we do this, we might not yet feel the pleasure of goodness. Consider this quote from Swedenborg:

> "The mountains into which they were to flee" means love to the Lord and consequent charity toward the neighbor. . . . Truth is said to turn away from good and look toward matters of doctrine when the member of the church no longer takes to heart what kind of life she or he leads, only what kind of doctrine she or he possesses. Yet it is life according to doctrine, not

---

1. Wilson Van Dusen, *Country of Spirit* (San Francisco: J. Appleseed & Co., 1992), 5–7.

> doctrine separate from life, that makes anyone a member of the
> church.   — *Secrets of Heaven* §2454 [4, 5]

Looking to life is what spiritual growth is all about. The quote above talks about those states in us that want to theorize and talk about the Work, but then when a negative state comes up, do not want to work. IT doesn't want to Work. IT just wants to talk about Work. So, of course, we need to flee from that state and instead find a Work I that is willing to Work, one that can work, one that does work.

Eventually, we *will* feel the pleasure of true good, when we enjoy Working.

The Task for Chapter 4

This time you get to pick which of two tasks you'd like to do.

Choice 1

The first option is to Work with someone else to get in touch with one of your negative recurring moods, a negative I. Have your Work partner interview you until that I has said everything on the subject it has to say, especially about how it feels, more than what it thinks, although you can let the I talk about what it thinks, too. After your negative I is finished speaking, switch and let the first interviewer be the interviewee and let his or her negative have a full say.

Before you try this, please know that it can be difficult to interview just one I. Sometimes when one negative I gets attention, any number of them line up and start interrupting each other. It does take some skill to keep focused. Your Work partner will begin to get a sense for that one particular I. If there are too many talking, he or she can gently tell the others to quiet down. If you interview too many negative I's at once, it is like being in a kindergarten room with a crowd of little children wanting to tell you things at once.

If you do this task, remember your Work partner will act as your Observing 'I'. Your intention in doing the task is to learn more about your negative 'I' and to listen for falsities in what it says.

Choice 2

The other task option is to notice when you are anticipating an event and then be aware of what actually happens. Suppose you are on your way to your job tomorrow morning and you have a quick flash of what the day is going to be like. Keep or remember that picture of your expectation, and then at the end of the day compare the picture you had with the reality of how things happened. Notice any similarities and any differences.

To do this task, you have to become aware of your projections, the pictures you have as you anticipate the future. Often such pictures are negative. If a holiday is approaching, perhaps you get a negative picture of the holiday as something you want to have over in a hurry. We all get pictures. Bring those projected pictures to your consciousness at the time of the actual event or afterwards. Then hold them side by side in your mind, and see how the two compare.

CHAPTER 5
Developing Your Aim

People in the stream of providence are being carried along constantly toward happier things, whatever appearance the means may present.

— *Emanuel Swedenborg*

Identifiying the Problem

If you went to your doctor for a physical and, after examining you, she said, "You are in bad shape. You really should do something about your health," you would want to know what exactly was wrong with you and what you should do. If you asked her for specifics and she responded, "I'm not sure, but you had better do something or you are going to be in deep trouble," you would probably feel very frustrated.

You might experience the same kind of frustration if you hired a plumber and he looked at your bathtub pipes and said, "You have a problem; your plumbing is in bad shape." You would say, "Well, what do you want to do?" If he said, "I don't know, but you need something," you would not feel very satisfied.

Now imagine a situation with a different response. Pretend you have a major appliance with something going wrong and you do not know exactly what is out of order. If a repairperson came to fix the appliance and, after looking at it, he said, "I know exactly what is wrong. I found this little wheel and one tooth of it is broken. All we have to do is replace the wheel; and, while I'm in there anyway, I can give you a brand new drive shaft, and then it's going to work fine again." You would feel better. The minute you get a report of exactly what the problem is and what has to be done about it, you would feel relieved. You would know what the problem is and what specifically has to be done to fix it.

In regard to their spiritual lives, a lot of people know that in general they are in bad shape and that they should be doing something about it, but they are not quite sure what it is they should be doing. They have an uneasy feeling.

In the last chapter, we considered recurring states of anxiety, solicitude about the future, worry, and concern. Because I frequently experience these kinds of states, I want to look at them and find something specific that I can Work on. What is wrong within me? In the case of anxiety, the next time I experience it I want to be aware of it and do something about it.

In order for me to focus on my anxiety and do something about it, I have to believe, for myself, that the problem is a spiritual issue. The effort isn't just something that I am going to work on because I would like to feel more at ease or relaxed. It is a spiritual issue because I believe there are spiritual forces involved, since everything is spiritual on some level.

However, it is important to distinguish between natural and spiritual temptations. There is a big difference between them.

When a natural temptation occurs, a natural love is being tempted. I might worry about a situation at my job, perhaps how I am going to get a report done on time. That is a natural love, a love of my paycheck and of reaching a goal in regard to it. But our natural or physical lives should serve our spiritual lives. Staying within a natural love keeps us at the lowest spiritual level possible, in our natural mind.

In contrast, the Work or heavenly influences try to elevate our mind and make us more useful on a higher level. Staying at the level of our natural mind when we want to be elevated constitutes a spiritual temptation. If we have the desire to be free from worldly concerns of time and space and want to rise to something spiritual but negative thoughts try to stop us, that is a temptation.

To be worrying and concerned about the future prevents the Lord from giving us true peace, trust, and contentment. If we are caught up in concerns on the natural level, the Lord can't give us those peaceful, higher states.

We must ask how the Lord wants us to deal with these kinds of problems, and then listen for the answers.

We have loves or affections or things we deeply care about, but sometimes we are not aware of them. Our affections (or intentions) reveal themselves through our thoughts. So we can get to know the nature of our will or active loves by means of observing our thoughts.

A person can elevate his or her thoughts to any height. What usually happens, however, is that the intellect is flying around at a very high altitude of elevated thinking, and then some lower natural love gets affronted, and the intellect comes falling down.

Here's an example: I came home from work and got ready to relax and watch television. My love for doing that was active and nothing was going against it, so I was very happy and relaxed. As I was about to turn on the television, one of my daughters came home and she also seemed content. My wife was about to go out to yoga and she was fine, too. Our thinking might have been somewhat elevated. All of a sudden my wife remembered that a younger daughter had to be driven to a driver's education class. She said to me, "Remember to drive her to class." Well! All of a sudden I felt anger, irritation, and negative thoughts that seemed true in my current state of mind. Why couldn't someone else drive her? My older daughter had her reason ready; she had to baby sit. My wife had her yoga class excuse. I thought, "This is the only night I don't have to go out counseling and it is *my* night to relax! I can only be happy and relax by watching television!"

Negative thoughts are automatic, and they have a false concept ready to express when a natural or selfish love is interfered with. Our elevated intellect suddenly drops down because of opposition. That high intellect does nothing for you, alone. The minute it is opposed, it drops down and serves selfish loves, instead of good loves. Your intellect doesn't fight to stay elevated. Someone asks you to do something, and IT says, "I work all week. I need a rest." And this sounds so reasonable, so true.

Swedenborg wrote that faith alone cannot save us spiritually. Truth all by itself cannot fight false conceptions, which are associated with evil. Only good can fight falsity, good from within the truth.

What does this mean? At the time of my intellect's dropping down to join a natural love, when it was time to drive my daughter to her driver's education class, the only thing I could do was to be aware that it was wrong to express anger and act from my negative thoughts. I could sort of freeze to refrain from doing anything negative. To freeze took a great deal of effort and Work. I wanted to express the negative; I felt those bad feelings. However, I was also aware of the good within the truth, aware that *good* was capable of not going along with the false ideas or believing them. That was all I was capable of, however, having that awareness and avoiding acting from the negative. I didn't have a sense of elevation or feel any good feelings, nor did I achieve full non-identification.

There is a big difference between a state of intellectual faith alone and a state in which good fights through truth. We cannot grow spiritually until we start living according to the truth or make that effort. Then good fights through truth, against the evil, which is fighting through falsehood. Here spiritual combat occurs, and here spiritual temptation is experienced. Here also Work takes place.

Although it feels bad to be in that kind of torment, actually we are freer, spiritually speaking, at that moment than we have ever been. Not being free is like floating down river toward the falls. We feel free if we don't try to swim upstream, but we are not free; our life is in danger. Spiritually, if we don't fight a negative thought, we feel free at the moment. When we fight, we do not feel free; rather we *feel* the torrent trying to carry us in a direction we don't want to go. Actually we are in more freedom than we have ever been because the Lord is fighting for us.

When we are in a negative state and try to Work by "freezing mid-fall," we should be aware of what is happening. The same is true when we are in a good state and a destructive thought appears. Remember the pharisee within us is always trying to interfere with genuine good. If we know that someone has a problem and we have a good inclination to call them on the phone, the pharisee in us comes and discourages us with some inconsequential excuse. The impulse to help is good, but a destructive thought appears saying it's not the right time to act.

You can notice and Work on those kinds of experiences.

Uses of Despair

Even if we've been Working for some time, we may have moments of despair. It's important to know that despair can be a necessary state on the way to a good state. There are bad states that are bad states, and then there are bad states that are just stages on the way to a good state.

Here's an analogy: I was on my way into Philadelphia and I saw construction workers rebuilding an old section of the city. You could tell good things were about to happen because this one house looked like a disaster. The roof had been taken off, all the paint was chipped, the windows were taken out, and the house had been stripped down to the bare essentials. It looked awful. I had been in that area before, and it had *looked* good before all that work, but it wasn't good; the wood was rotten, the paint was peeling. But now the house was reduced to what could be rebuilt. I thought that maybe some despair was involved when the house was first dismantled in preparation for repair. The Lord allows these things for a purpose. The tearing down process is necessary.

A lot of people try to avoid the stage of despair by being active in external things like taking vacations, medicating themselves, or just doing whatever they can to avoid the experience of despair. But the Lord says we have to come to that kind of experience before we can be led. In order for us to be willing to let the Lord lead us, we have to despair of our negative states and become empty of them before we can be rebuilt or refilled. Feeling empty is a terrible feeling; but if we are being emptied in order to be refilled, then it is worth it.

However, there will be a period of time during which we feel empty and say to ourselves, "I give up. I am only trying to grow spiritually because the Lord said to. I am not getting any good feelings out of it yet, but I'll just do it for his sake." The last bit of self-serving has to go, even the idea of the pay-off, the happiness of heaven. The part of us that Works obediently (without enjoying it) can lead us for a ways toward spiritual growth, but it is not the contented state we will have when we are able to Work more eagerly.

Hopelessness is just another negative emotion. If you experience it, you might find it lingers with you. Just observe it. Try to not identify with it. Ask the Lord how to look at it from a spiritual standpoint. You will feel hopeless, but you can know intellectually that you are not. Start to get distance. Think, "IT is hopeless, but I don't have to be."

The Importance of Trust

One thing of great value we may have been given as children was to be taught passages from religious books so that we memorized them and thereby built up a storehouse of sayings in our minds. As adults, we can bring to mind the truths we need at any moment.

I find the following biblical passages useful for getting clear about worry, anxiety, and solicitude, and what the Lord wants us to do. Perhaps you have heard these quotes so many times that you will read or hear them again through your memory. Instead, try to hear them brand new.

Before reading the quotes, just relax for a moment and let something come to mind that you have been concerned or anxious about this week. Now, think of one more thing that has concerned you lately. And now look backward to a month ago, noticing if either worry was there at that time. Now see a month from now in the future; perhaps the worries are much dimmer in that future. Now see from a perspective of five years from now, or even ten years from now . . . And now, as you let those concerns go, just bring to mind a phrase or sentence from divine revelation in regard to your being some way the Lord suggests, or asks, or tells you to be. Recall a helpful, wise, or comforting phrase, a phrase that is telling you something your Heavenly Father wants you to know and remember. Take your time. Let the phrase or phrases float into your consciousness, until you notice them and recall them in thought or words. When you are fully ready, you may begin reading:

"Do not store up for yourselves treasures on earth, where moth and rust consume and where thieves break in and steal; but store up for yourselves treasures in heaven, where neither moth nor rust consumes and where thieves do not break in and steal. For where your treasure is, there your heart will be also."   — Matthew 6:19–21

"No one can serve two masters; for a slave will either hate the one and love the other, or be devoted to the one and despise the other. You cannot serve God and wealth.

"Therefore I tell you, do not worry about your life, what you will eat or what you will drink, or about your body, what you will wear. Is not life more than food, and the body more than clothing?"   — Matthew 6:24–25

"And can any of you by worrying add a single hour to your span of life? And why do you worry about clothing? Consider the lilies of the field, how they grow; they neither toil nor spin, yet I tell you, even Solomon in all his glory was not clothed like one of these."   — Matthew 6:27–29

> "Therefore do not worry, saying, 'What will we eat?' or
> 'What will we drink?' or 'What will we wear?' For it is the
> Gentiles who strive for all these things; and indeed your heav-
> enly Father knows that you need all these things. But strive
> first for the kingdom of God and his righteousness, and all these
> things will be given to you as well.
>
> "So do not worry about tomorrow, for tomorrow will bring
> worries of its own. Today's trouble is enough for today."
>
> — Matthew 6:31–34

When you choose between the I's or states in yourself, you
want to distinguish between the purely natural or physical
states (the "What am I to eat and drink?" states) from those
that are seeking something higher. You can locate a higher
state and move toward it.

Swedenborg wrote about two types of people: those who
worry or have solicitude about the future and those who are
unconcerned and unruffled.

> People are concerned about the morrow when they are not con-
> tent with their lot, do not trust in God but in themselves, and
> have solely worldly and earthly things in view, not heavenly
> ones. These people are ruled completely by anxiety over the
> future, and by the desire to possess all things and exercise
> control over all other people.   — Secrets of Heaven §8478[2]

When Swedenborg refers to people who are "concerned
about the morrow," he is not talking about other people; he is
talking about states in you and me. You will notice and hear
states in yourself that are concerned only with worldly things.
Those states will be active in you, and they have no concern
for the Work, no concern for spiritual things. You will feel
their sphere.

> Those who trust in the Divine are altogether different.
> Though concerned about the morrow, still they are uncon-
> cerned, in that they are not anxious, let alone worried, when

they give thought to the morrow. They remain even-tempered whether or not they realize their desires, and they do not grieve over loss; they are content with their lot. . . . They know that for those who trust in the Divine all things are moving toward an everlasting state of happiness, and that no matter what happens at any time to them, it contributes to that state.

It should be recognized that Divine providence is over all, that is, it is present within the smallest details of all, and that people in the stream of providence are being carried along constantly toward happier things, whatever appearance the means may present. Those in the stream of providence are people who trust in the Divine and ascribe everything to him. But those not in the stream of providence are people who trust in themselves alone and attribute everything to themselves. . . . It should be recognized also that to the extent that anyone is in the stream of providence he or she is in a state of peace. . . . These alone know and believe that the Lord's Divine providence resides within every single thing, indeed within the smallest details of all.   — *Secrets of Heaven* §8478[3, 4]

The passages from Swedenborg's *Secrets of Heaven* make it clear that solicitude about tomorrow and anxiety are states where negative thoughts attack. Those particular I's in us are concerned for tomorrow, but there is another state available to us if we are in the stream of providence. When Swedenborg refers to people "in the stream of providence" he *doesn't* say "only people who have grown spiritually" or "only people who are in the Work"; he *does* say "people who trust in the Divine and ascribe everything to him."

So when something goes wrong with a report you are doing, when you forget to put in a correct item, when your child spills a glass of milk, in all of the most minute details of your life, the Lord is present and he is taking care of you in every way that entails your spiritual welfare. If you really trust him down to the most minute detail, then whatever state you are in, the good and truth within that state is capable of bringing you peace.

Now, of course, when a selfish love is activated, when you don't get your way, when someone doesn't say hello or breaks something important to you, or you don't get somewhere on time, and a negative state is active, that is when you might seek and ask for a saying from divine revelation. It is very powerful during a temptation to ask for a phrase from divine revelation. In the Work, this is referred to as "bringing the Work to incoming impressions." At the time a negative state is active, ask what you have learned from divine revelation about this. What have you learned, what does the church teach, that applies to this state in you? It may take effort and attention to think of a truth right then. But even if you just bring to mind the fact that the Lord is in everything most minute that is occurring no matter what the appearance, you will know that whatever you are experiencing is for your eternal spiritual welfare. If you bring a religious truth to the state, you can move toward a feeling of peace.

The Lord is asking us to make an effort. He cannot give us feelings of peace if we remain in the states of worldly and corporeal concerns. If that is where we are residing, he cannot reach us. He will just stand at the door and knock.

Spiritual growth cannot be just an intellectual process. In the Work, it is said, "The Work must become emotional." When negative I's are active and change seems impossible, that is the time you have to Work. And if you Work at that time, emotions are involved. You really feel the love that you have of being free of evil, and you are emotionally involved in the struggle. Then the influence of the Work can stay with you. If you try to Work without being emotionally involved, its influence is not really with you. You may have the Work in your memory for a time—you may fly along thinking lofty thoughts, but when a selfish love hits, you will come down and get stuck in the mire.

"Being emotional" means that your intent (or will) is involved. When you have an active negative state and refuse to go along with the false assumptions, when you refuse to act from that selfish state, it takes will and determination. If you just go along with a negative inclination, you might look back two days later and say, "Oh yes, that's when I should have Worked!"

Swedenborg wrote that only good can fight evil, that truth by itself cannot fight evil. There is no will or intent involved when you yield to a negative. There is just a truth being destroyed by an evil as you give in.

Developing a Specific Aim

Consider something as concrete as your plumber saying, "I found this one little washer that has been causing the problem, and it has to be replaced." You ask the plumber what has to be done next. Then you are told exactly what has to be done. "I have to go to the store and buy this size washer, then I have to take the cap off and place the washer inside." The plumber explains what the next step is, and that step is very specific.

In a spiritual effort, we also should have at least one specific aim or goal—not a far aim, but one particular aim concerning one specific evil. We find a particular evil in ourselves, and we want to have a plan for when that evil recurs.

Whether we plan to use nonjudgmental self-observation or to hold the negative state side by side with a phrase from divine revelation or to "stop thought" is not critical. Just have some aim or plan. It doesn't matter whether it turns out to be the best aim or whether you do it well. What does matter is that you have an aim, and when negative I's appear you make the effort to carry out your aim. Even if you just ask the Lord for some phrase from his Word, that is having an aim.

If you want to see how well repetition works, get on a unicycle. The judgmental mind can't ride a unicycle. It gives up. When a child gets on a unicycle, he or she says it is impossible. But all you really have to do is just keep getting on, even though you fall off every time. If you keep getting on and falling off, eventually that getting on and falling off will teach you how to ride a unicycle!

It is the same with having an aim. It doesn't matter whether your aim is great or insightful, minor or major; if you *use it*, the process of using it will teach you how to make corrections and how to start improving. Taking some action will change your aim and make it a better aim, a more correct aim.

But what if you have no aim? If the Work is just theoretical for you and you have no plan of attack, you can't ride a unicycle, spiritually speaking. You cannot learn to ride a unicycle by studying it. *You have to get on it and do it.* And I am not talking about the general aim of growing spiritually. I am talking about working on one specific thing in your own spiritual life, focusing on one specific evil that you will to Work on. As Maurice Nicoll explains,

> Now unless we have some kind of aim the Work cannot influ-
> ence our lives for then we are not surrounded by the Work, but
> remain open to all the influences of life. . . . If we remember our
> aim in the midst of life we feel at once that two quite different
> things are acting on us . . . . This is giving acknowledgment and
> so power to the Work. It may be only a transient experience but
> yet it is a very genuine one, and although it may eventually fail
> we at least get the taste for a moment of what it might mean to
> stand within the influences of the Work. . . .[1]

---

1. Nicoll, *Commentaries*, 907.

❦

The Task for Chapter 5

Once again, we have two choices.

Choice 1

Our first task is to become aware of anxiety and worry regarding the future, and then to compare that with a religious phrase. Whenever solicitude arrives, become aware of it, and immediately see if you can recall some phrase from divine revelation. Hold the solicitude and the phrase side by side. Do this every time you worry about the future.

Choice 2

The other task option is to become aware of coveting. Here's an example from my own life. I was driving down a country road, looking at the river coursing alongside the road. I also saw beautiful houses. I observed that I could not appreciate the lovely view fully because I wanted everything I saw. I wanted every little house, every big house, every doghouse. Coveting was a negative experience, and I could not appreciate the view because of the wanting experience. The self wanted it all.

"Thou shalt not covet," the commandment says. The word covet is often mentioned in the Bible, and we want to become aware of what it is in our lives, how it feels, and how we would go about giving it up in order to become content with our lot. The next time you covet something, try to avoid it. You might try to "stop thought" completely. If you succeed, you will not be able to think of what you were coveting. Or, you could just say the phrase to yourself, "Thou shalt not covet," and see what that does to your pattern of coveting while you are experiencing it. Ask the question, "What is coveting for me?" Then when you experience coveting, remember that the Lord does not want us to covet.

CHAPTER 6
Directing the Natural to Serve the Spiritual

When a man begins to apply this Work practically to himself he begins, as it were, to fly a little above the surface of the earth.

— *Maurice Nicoll*

How do you grow spiritually? The answer is one word: *actually*.

I recall as a young athlete, talking about doing a certain type of dive, thinking about doing that dive, and then standing up on the diving board looking down thirty feet, and finally *actually* jumping up in the air and diving. When we go into action and *actually* do something, things change.

To actually do something is taking a step from what is known into what is unknown. I know how to think about a new dive, and I know how to talk about it; but when I jump up into the air, I'm not sure whether I know how to *do it* or not.

In psychiatry they speak about people having dysfunctional behavior. Take a student who always hands in her work late. She gets a lot of negative feedback about this behavior, so why does she keep doing it? She could get her work in on time and get positive feedback. The answer is that she knows how to deal with failure. She knows how to deal with a teacher's being angry because the student has been in that situation often. She doesn't, however, know how to deal with success. For the most part, people would rather deal with the known than with the unknown.

In the Bible, we are given different descriptions of the Promised Land. The Israelites were told they would leave Egypt for a land flowing with milk and honey (Exodus 3:8), while Revelation 21:21 describes a place where the streets are paved with gold. Today, spiritually, we don't actually know the kinds of wonderful places described in the Bible. We have heard about states of peace, confidence, and friendship, but how often have we experienced them in the spiritual fullness that is possible? To a great degree, they are unknown to us. On the other hand, we certainly know about the sensual world we live in every day, about being angry or irritated or feeling superior and contemptuous toward our neighbor. We all know about negative feelings. Yet we are asked to start taking a trip toward better spiritual states. So when we begin to Work, we are embarking on a journey toward the unknown, a trip toward something we have heard about but have not experienced.

Why Letting Go of Negativity Is So Difficult

The Israelites didn't like being slaves in Egypt. When they were told they were to leave, they knew that they were going to the Promised Land. Still, the Israelites were aware that they were moving from a known situation to something unknown.

A while after the Israelites left Egypt, they were stumbling along in the desert, and they reacted with dissatisfaction and complained to Moses and Aaron:

> The whole congregation of the Israelites complained against Moses and Aaron in the wilderness. The Israelites said to them, "If only we had died by the hand of the LORD in the land of Egypt, when we sat by the fleshpots and ate our fill of bread; for you have brought us out into this wilderness to kill this whole assembly with hunger."   — Exodus 16:2–3

Out in the desert, spiritually speaking, when you don't know the way, there is a space between the leaving of what is known, although negative, and arriving in the Promised Land.

Self-observation shows us where we live now in a spiritual regard. As we start to see our negative states, increasingly we see some reason for wanting to leave the place or state of mind we are in. But when we begin the journey, and we do some Work and we start resisting our negative mechanical states, do we feel satisfied right away? Do we immediately feel the joy of doing good? Do we immediately feel love toward our neighbors? No, we do not.

When we begin to Work, we are traveling in the desert. We are between where we were and where we will eventually be. And we have to be in the desert for a substantial length of time before we reach the Promised Land because, if we left the Egypt of our dysfunction and immediately entered the Promised Land, the *self* would feel gratified. If we left behind the delights of feeling superior to the neighbor and immediately had the pleasure of loving the neighbor, the self would get into that feeling and take merit for it.

There needs to be an emptying out of the self, a state where we give up all the delights of self and then for a time just Work from pure faith and obedience. During this time, we are leaving the known, leaving the senses, "dying" to the self, and living in a state of negativity that feels like our life but from which we do not act. We have to give up something we know well (such as a recurring negative)—which feels like we are giving up our known life—for something we have been told about but have not experienced.

But, after we get to a state of actually Working and we approach the unknown, we will develop a sense that the end is worth the struggle. We also develop a clearer understanding that there really is such a thing as a spiritual life and that faith in the Lord will sustain us.

The Lord is telling us to work toward spiritual growth. It was not Moses who had the idea of leaving Egypt. The Lord told

Moses to go, and the Lord said he would put the words in Moses's mouth to tell the people. It was really the Lord speaking (Exodus 3–4).

When we become passive to our selfish will, we allow a new will to become alive. When we start to become passive to our negative I's, we do that because of truths in our rational minds. As we elevate our minds, we gain good to join with those truths.

Swedenborg wrote that heavenly joy is almost impossible to describe (*Heaven and Hell* §398). That indescribable joy is the goal; it is why we are leaving Egypt, spiritually speaking. The Lord really wishes to give us something he calls "the Promised Land." The Lord wishes to give us joy to replace the negative delights of IT. That joy is the result of Working.

Listening to the Lord's Words

What kind of subjects easily grab your attention? If I read an article from a tabloid newspaper to you, I could probably keep your interest without any problem, because the lowest level of your mind would be drawn to what I was reading. No effort or attention would be needed on your part.

Now if I had a manual on computer operation and started reading that to you, I probably would lose you completely. But if you had just purchased a computer, then I might be able to interest you. So, let's say you just purchased a computer and have been struggling to understand it. Let's say your computer keeps crashing every time you turn it on and you just don't understand why. Then, if I started reading the manual on that very problem, perhaps you would listen with a rapt intensity! You would be learning to actually operate your computer.

When we read from divine revelation, we read about actual events that will be taking place in our spiritual lives, *if* we choose to go along the paths that the Lord wishes us to go and to receive the joys that he wishes to give to us. In divine revelation, the Lord is telling you what is going on in your soul, or will be going on, when you get to that stage. He has already told you about the thoughts and the feelings you have (like feeling superior to someone) and about the negatives you struggle with (like doubt), so it may come to your attention that he knows you pretty well. He talks about what you know in the quiet of your own heart, and he tells you things that no one else could know. So when he starts to tell you about the unknown, you can feel assured that he is describing something real, even if you haven't experienced it yet.

The Lord doesn't talk to us as a flamboyant speaker, and divine revelation doesn't read much like a tabloid newspaper. The part of your mind that likes tabloid newspapers—the lower, natural part—would not want to go hear the Lord's words.

But the part of your mind that he wants to communicate with is the part that actually is struggling with spiritual growth. When you are in an active negative state, that part is suffering and confused, and it doesn't know why you keep hurting the people you love or why you keep doing things that you know are wrong. That part of the mind is not going to go listen to the tabloid news, no matter how entertaining or amusing; it will instead go running to where it can listen to the Lord's words.

When I go to church, no matter how wonderful the minister's sermon is, I still prefer to hear a reading from divine revelation. Then, no matter who is reading or how they sound, I know it is our Lord talking. He is talking to us about the actual spiritual journey we are each taking right now. The Creator of the Universe is talking to you and to me about the things that our very lives depend on! You can't ask for more than that.

Remember that we each have a natural mind, a rational mind, and a spiritual mind. Remember the monologues inside our heads and our pictures of the future and how our natural minds think. It appears to us that the external world of space and time can cause our reactions, our frustrations, our irritations, etc. The reality is that, on the spiritual plane, there is no space, there is no time, and all causes are internal.

The more we progress spiritually, the more we will come to see that spiritual thought is not in words. Spiritual things are perceived in an entirely different way from natural things. When we quiet our minds, we will not be hearing the kind of things we have been hearing from our negative I's. Swedenborg explains this:

> Sense impressions put us in touch with the world, rational notions in touch with heaven. . . . If our thought is not raised above the level of sense impressions, our wisdom is very restricted. When our thought is raised above this level, we come into brighter illumination, and eventually into the light of heaven, so that then we can perceive such ideas as flow down from heaven. . . . Sense impressions should occupy the last place, not the first. In the case of a wise and intelligent person they do come last and are subject to what is more interior. But in the case of an unwise person they occupy the first place and dominate him or her.   — *True Christian Religion* §565[3]

One scholar of Swedenborg's writings explains how our external and interior minds operate during our lifetime:

> What is transacted in the rational mind is "unknown to the natural, for it is above the sphere of its observation.". . .
> [W]ith the well-disposed, and especially those who are being regenerated, the Rational has been interiorly opened, and serves as the basis of the Spiritual Mind and also of the Celestial Mind. . . . The general doctrine therefore is, that while in the world man "thinks both spiritually and naturally, but does not apperceive those things which he thinks spiritually.". . . As every man has a spiritual mind, as well as a natural mind, "it cannot be but that both minds think" . . . but because the spiritual mind lies hid in the natural mind or lives above it, man is wholly unaware of what he thinks in that mind. . . .
> This is the reason why all spiritual purification must be effected in the natural mind while man is on earth: for only

there do his states, his thoughts and affections, "come to mani-
fest perception." . . . In states of spiritual enlightenment man
can however to some little extent perceive truths . . . which can
hardly be expressed in human words. . . .[1]

As long as we keep love of the Lord at the top of our
priorities, we have nothing to worry about. The goal is to
subjugate our natural mind and make it subservient to our
spiritual mind so that the natural serves instead of dominates.
If our natural mind serves our spiritual goals, it is harmless and
is a friend. If it rules and dominates, it is an enemy.

Odhner further describes the process of subjugating the lower
natural mind to the higher spiritual:

[T]he Spiritual Mind, or Spiritual Degree, within man, is
opened when by repentance man abstains from evils as sins and,
within his rational mind, receives spiritual truths from a love
of them for their own sake, and sees them in their own light,
acknowledging that they are from the Lord alone. . . . [A]nd
[man] then consents to a new creative operation by the Lord,
who begins to make man's spirit such as man prayerfully
desires himself to be and yet knows that he is not and could
never by his own endeavor become. . . .

[T]he reformation of the natural mind is likened to the
twisting back of a spiral into a reverse direction; which
requires considerable labor. . . . For the quirks and inhibitions,
the self-centered [desires] and subterfuges and passions of the
natural man, must be put away and cleaned out, and room made
for "natural" good affections from the Rational, which can
serve and obey the purposes of heaven. New delights must be
established in the natural—and old delights subjugated and
reduced to impotence or servitude.[2]

---

1. Hugo Lj. Odhner, *The Human Mind* (Bryn Athyn, Pa.: Swedenborg Scientific
Association, 1969), 97–98. Reprinted by permission.
2. Odhner, 98–100.

We can only work with what we perceive, and perception takes place in our natural mind. But actually, our spiritual growth is being done by the Lord alone. As we make efforts within our natural minds, such as by trying to quiet a negative, chattering monologue, the Lord is doing the Work for us in the most spiritual parts of our minds. When we cleanse the negative or evil tendencies of our natural minds and make them subservient or passive, we will begin to receive different and more spiritual kinds of ideas and feelings because our reception of heavenly things will improve.

Spiritual Trust and Natural Trust

Sometimes we may contemplate withdrawing from worldly concerns so that we can focus on heavenly things. We might ask the Lord, "Well, what about this world? I've got a job, a spouse, and two children. Don't I have to worry about them?" The Lord says, "All these things will be given to you as well" (Matthew 6:33). In Matthew 6:32, the Lord says, in effect, "I know you need a job, and clothes, and food, etc. I know you need all these things, but look at the lilies." Think of him and his goals for you. He is indicating that he *is* taking care of things for us. If we do what he tells us to do—put spiritual goals before natural ones—we will be amazed at what he takes care of for us! He clothes the lilies, and he takes care of the birds. Don't you think we are more important to him than the birds? He knows they need nests; he knows we need a place to live, but he is trying to give us things that are far more important than a place to live, although he is not going to leave that undone. He wants to give us the assurance that we are much more important than the birds.

It takes a lot of trust to believe that. Pride in our own intelligence and lust for power get in the way. We have taken upon ourselves this awful burden of our lives that we can't carry or handle. The Lord is trying to take that burden off us again, and he asks in Matthew 6:25–26 why we have taken on the total responsibility when he is going to do it for us. But the natural mind doubts. That is why Peter sank in the water (Matthew 14:29–30). Peter fell down into the concerns of the world, into time and space.

Swedenborg wrote:

> People necessarily incur guilt if they believe they are acting of themselves, whether it is good or evil that they do. But they do not incur guilt if they believe they are acting as if of themselves. For if they believe that they do good of themselves, they are claiming for themselves what belongs to God; and if they believe that they do evil of themselves, they are attributing to themselves what belongs to the devil.
>
> — *True Christian Religion* §621[10]

Heaven is not a place where nothing negative shows up in us. Heaven is a state where, through the process of spiritual growth, negatives are brought up, seen, and admitted, and we pray to the Lord to have them removed. Gradually we become passive to the negatives. Actually, each negative keeps popping up again and again, but it becomes finer and finer, meaning less gross. Even in heavenly states, the negative has not been fully removed, but it has become quiescent.

Have you ever noticed that, when you concentrate on something that you already know how to do by rote, like shifting gears or opening a letter, that you don't do it well? Your natural mind knows how to do it better than your intellectual mind does, and your natural mind will be a better driver than you will be trying to do it from a conscious awareness long after you've learned how to do it. There is a part of your mind that can even do your job at work just as well as it can drive your car (unless you are brand new at work and are just learning your duties).

Even though all this is true, we are so mechanical that we often spend all day focusing on our natural, external lives.

There's a story a Sufi teacher told about a man who was taking a train ride. The man got on the train, and as he traveled, he held onto his luggage although it was very heavy. He had a bag in his right hand, a bag in his left hand, and a bag under each arm. Someone on the train asked him why he was holding his luggage. He said, "I need my luggage, so I hold on to it. I have to make sure it travels, too. I need my baggage!" It made perfect sense to him.

I knew a woman named Sally, who wanted to learn to play the piano. She didn't have any music, or a teacher, or even a piano, so she went and bought herself a player-piano. She plugged it in and tried to follow the keys wherever they moved, and eventually she got better at following the keys. After five or six years, she could hit each one as it went down. She started playing that player-piano in a cafe she purchased. One day some of her old friends from high school came into the cafe, and one of them invited Sally over to visit with them. Sally said, "No, I can't. I have to keep playing the piano. I have to entertain the people here." Her friends said, "You don't have to play that piano!" But Sally said, "Yes. Oh, yes, I do. I have to make the music and entertain the people."

Now, you probably do not spend much time concentrating on making your heart beat. When I was a child, I was terrified when I went to sleep. I was afraid my heart would stop. I would listen and my heart kept going, but I was always afraid that I might hear it stop. Finally I noticed that I did not have any control over it! So then I gave up and let it beat away, as it still does.

You probably do not pay much attention to your breathing, either, although you could. You could stop breathing, you could do shallow breathing, you could breathe deeply, or you could not pay any attention to your breathing and you would still breathe! You don't pay much attention to your cells either, do you? You do not make them operate or grow, and yet they do both. You feel life as your own, even though you do not run your heart, or your lungs, and you don't make your cells active. Yet they still feel like your own, do they not? Your whole body feels like it belongs to you.

In a similar manner, our natural, corporeal, sensual mind is also not under our control. We could actually get up tomorrow, go to work, go to school, get the children off to where they need to go, cook a meal, get in the car and drive it, ride a bicycle, and do all kinds of things without thinking about it. Our "machine" can handle all of our natural life without our paying one bit of attention to it whatsoever. But if you want to carry your luggage . . . if you want to play the player-piano . . . feel free. But keep in mind this next story about a man named Joe.

Joe owned a small company. He had complete control of it, and it was a good company, a one-man operation. Joe did the ordering, made the machinery, did the typing, the selling, and the billing. He made the phone calls. He did it all, and he did a great job.

Another businessman noticed that Joe's company was a good one, so he bought it, hiring Joe as part of the deal. The new owner gave Joe the title of chief executive and greatly expanded the company and hired many new employees. Now the company made 500,000 widgets a day instead of 1,000. Joe sat in his big office.

One day Joe had a great idea and went to the secretary and said, "Will you please move out of the way? I need to write a letter." So he typed out a letter telling a new client that the company would send them 15,000 widgets. Then Joe went down to the stamping machine and asked several workers to move out of the way so he could make some widgets. Meanwhile, his secretary, having less to do now, went into Joe's office and started answering the phone and making big decisions. The workers in the factory started drinking and playing cards. Joe got an ulcer.

This story shows that a newly expanded company can go one of two ways. Either the boss can start delegating and the business will function smoothly, or the boss can control everything and find that the business will get into trouble. The boss must delegate, and in order to do that he or she must be able to *trust*. If the boss tells an employee to type a letter or stamp out a product, the boss has to trust that the letter will be typed or the stamping done.

Just so, we have to trust our natural minds to take care of our natural lives. We don't have to wonder or worry about what we are going to do tomorrow on the natural plane. We were given a natural mind to take care of that part of our life so that we can devote ourselves to a higher state of existence.

Why would you want to have your spiritual mind driven by your natural mind, which is like a player-piano? The natural mind is a machine. Do you really want your spiritual mind dominated by a machine, when that very machine was created to serve your spiritual mind?

The Task for Chapter 6

This task is about delegating. Delegate your entire natural life to your natural mind/machine for a week. You might ask, "How do I do that?" Well, don't give it another thought. That is how you do it! *Don't give it another thought.* Trust your secretary; she knows how to type. Typing is part of her job. Trust your machine operator; he knows how to make widgets. Trust the billing clerk; he can bill. Delegate! Your natural mind will write your lists and take your knowledge and weed the garden for you. Remember that you are *not* your natural mind; you just happen to *have* one, and it can work for you in managing your external life.

As you do the task, you may find yourself writing a list, and that's okay. But if you are doing the task correctly, you will find your natural mind writing the list and prioritizing that lower level of your life, if you let it. After the big plan is in place, just let your machine do its work and you can watch. *Just don't give it another thought.* Your natural mind already is doing it; you just think you are doing it, like the woman playing the player-piano.

You might ask, "What will I do with my time?" Do as it says in Matthew 6:25 and 6:33: "Do not worry about your life, what you will eat or what you will drink, what you will wear. . . . Strive first for the kingdom of God." Delegate everything natural to your natural mind, and think spiritually. Your machine will pay your bills and organize your mind if you butt out and tend instead to your spiritual life. You can put your attention on your spirituality rather than focus on natural concerns all day long.

Another way of doing the task is to "stop thought." But the task really is not just stopping thought; it is trusting that your natural life is going to be cared for by your natural mind. Experiment. You have all had twenty or thirty years of being in charge, right? So take a week and delegate.

Once in a while when I wake up in the morning my machine says, "It's Monday, so you should . . ." but I don't give it another thought, because I don't have to think right then about what weekday it is or what is scheduled. When I get to my desk at work, there is a calendar and it shows me that this is Monday and Jim Swartz will be in at nine o'clock. My natural mind knows that fact already and probably wants me to start worrying a few hours early, but I don't have to do that. What a big relief to find out that it all handles itself if I let it.

Don't let emotions have their way. The chief executive should remain in charge of emotions. The boss makes the big decisions. If a negative emotion comes along and tries to take over the company, then the boss should come in and say, "Oh, no. Everyone back to his or her work stations. It's my job to handle emotions." So think spiritually, and Work on your emotions.

CHAPTER 7
Freedom from Natural Time

Predictions about the future and memories of the past are what
take away all pleasure and happiness in life.
                                        —*Emanuel Swedenborg*

*I*f you can, imagine someone who has come to a state
where she believes that the Lord takes care of everything,
that the Lord leads to all good. You can imagine that person
living life with a tremendous amount of confidence. She would
live very fluidly, very responsibly. She would look like she had
self-confidence, but she would really have confidence in the
Lord.

Someone else may have a great deal of *self*-confidence, but
none in the Lord. When we say "self-confidence," we mean a
false confidence in IT. So in the case of someone with much
self-confidence but none in the Lord, there would be fear and
anxiety under the veneer of apparent confidence.

Giving up confidence in IT does not mean that you go
around without any confidence; giving up confidence in IT
means that your confidence is placed in the Lord. And when
there is confidence in the Lord, there is a state of peace.
Confidence in the Lord changes your overall attitude from
negativity to hope.

Swedenborg described this state as one of tranquility:

> Peace holds within itself trust in the Lord, the trust that he
> governs all things and provides all things, and that he leads
> toward an end that is good. When we believe these things
> about him we are at peace, since we fear nothing and no anxiety
> about things to come disturbs us. How far we attain this state
> depends on how far we come to love the Lord. Everything bad,
> especially trust in ourselves, robs us of the state of peace.
>   — *Secrets of Heaven* §8455 [1, 2]

We have to Work from a positive attitude. You may have
heard about positive doubt and negative doubt. A positive
attitude about the Work is basically being willing to do the
Work, even wanting to do it. A positive attitude does not
come from a feeling such as *I'd better do the Work*, or *I should
do the Work*. Such attitudes are diametrically opposed to a
positive attitude about the Work.

Imagine that a child comes up to you and gives you a gift.
If the child has been told that he or she has to give you a gift
because you are a relative, receiving it does not feel very good.
On the other hand, if the child really wants to give you a gift,
you feel the sweetness and love in it. You know from buying
presents yourself that, if you buy something because you feel
you "should" you have one feeling; if you do it because you
really want to give a special gift to someone, you experience
an entirely different feeling. Doing the Work is our gift to the
Lord.

Both Swedenborg's writings and the Work stress how little
our efforts at change mean unless they are done as a free-will
offering. As we sacrifice our negative life, we struggle and fight
against our selfish loves, and that work needs to be done from
our free will. What we render unto the Lord should be from
freedom that comes from our love to the Lord.

Time Is an Appearance, But Eternity Is Spiritual

Time is subjective. It seems short sometimes and long at other times. As an extreme example, Milton Erikson, the great hypnotist, sometimes suggests that a client take a new look at his life from childhood on up to the present. The client, while in a trance, is invited to relive their entire life at the same speed they lived it, and yet Dr. Erikson gives them only ten seconds within which to do that, and they do it! They seem to relive their life at the same speed as it was lived previously, but they do it in ten seconds of time! So time can be distorted.

Swedenborg wrote that there is no time in the next world and that our spiritual lives even now do not operate in time or space. But what application does this have to the Work? What application does it have to our lives in the physical world? It has a great deal of application.

> When we are in a state of love or heavenly feelings, we are in an angelic state—that is, a state in which time does not seem to exist—as long as there is no impatience in our feelings. Impatience is an emotion created by our bodies. So far as we feel impatient, we are subject to the constraints of time; but so far as impatience does not enter into our feelings, we are free of time's constraints. . . . The feelings that go with genuine love draw us away from bodily and worldly concerns because they lift our minds toward heaven. In the process they draw us away from any notion of time.　　　—*Secrets of Heaven* §3827

We usually think about time as occurring in a line. We speak of being *on* time and of some event taking place *within* the hour. But this is an illusion. Although the natural mind seems to live in time, this is actually just an appearance. Imagine a line with another line crossing it:

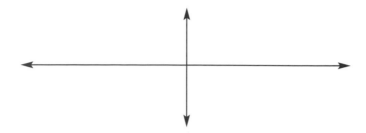

Maurice Nicoll says that where we exist at this very moment is where eternity, which is pictured as vertical, crosses our horizontal time line. No matter where you are on the horizon, the vertical is present. Eternity *is* whereas time just *appears to be*. Time is an illusion, an appearance where eternity crosses it.

There is no time or space in eternity; eternity is spiritual. We can say that to the degree a person is drawn away from bodily things, to that degree the person has an experience of being in life but not *of* life. Maurice Nicoll explains how timelessness applies to the Work:

> [O]ne definition that Christ gave of God [is] that with God all things are possible. God is not in Time but in Eternity, outside Time, having nothing to do with Time. That is why, in order to understand aright what is above us, we have to get rid of Time in our thoughts. We have to get away from Time altogether in order to reach a level of ourselves that is above us. Time and space prevent us from reaching a possible and actually existing higher level of ourselves. A man must be re-born out of Time and Space—for his mind, if awakened, can understand and reach to a higher dimensional world in which there is no Time and all *is*—not was. . . . The past *is*—not *was*—and so can be changed. *I can change my past by working on myself now.* . . . Among other things you begin to think in a new way if you think of passing time as an illusion.[1]

---

1. Nicoll, *Commentaries*, 951.

We each have a natural mind, but we are not that natural
mind. We can experience our lives more fully than just
experiencing our natural minds existing in time and space. We
are told to go beyond the natural and seek the kingdom of
heaven. To do this, we must elevate ourselves out of time and
out of space. How do we do that? The ultimate answer is to
know that there is nothing important except spiritual growth,
cleansing ourselves, and bringing ourselves to loving the Lord
and loving the neighbor. These are the only things of real
importance.

Of course, our selfish loves are striving to make other things
seem more important than spiritual growth. It takes effort to be
elevated. But to the degree that we do become elevated, to
that degree we enter eternity, the spiritual state where time
and space do not exist. When we are there, life is our teacher.
When a bad experience approaches, just say, *Here comes the
teacher!* Life becomes a means rather than an end in itself.

For example, sometime in the future, you may feel a sudden
desire to buy something or to own something that you do not
need. On the strictly natural level or time line, you would go
ahead and buy it. On the eternity line, that desire to buy is a
means by which you can be elevated as you reject acting upon it.

We know the Bible says that we should not put our hearts
on riches. We know we should not treasure things that moth
and rust destroy, that thieves break in and steal (Matthew
6:19). But how do we know where our treasure is? We can
know by finding out what upsets us, by finding out what we
spend our time thinking about, and by finding where our
emotions and concerns are involved. That is where our heart
is, where our treasure is.

We might say, "Oh, I don't consider gold a treasure. I don't
put my heart on that." The Lord isn't talking about gold as
gold. He's talking about the natural, material delights of the
world like a car, a house, a job, even arriving on time for a
date—all natural space- and time-oriented things. Are those
the things about which you get upset? If so, recognize it as your

natural mind operating at the natural level. That is where your heart is, that is where moth and rust corrupt, that is where thieves break through and steal.

Becoming aware of our attachments to things within time and space can give us some indication of where we are in the Work. We can notice where we are putting our attention, our thoughts and our emotions. To be elevated from space and time is to be lifted out of hellish lives toward more heavenly states.

We want to get out of time and space as soon and as often as possible. If we live in time and space, then our life is a pharaoh, a tyrant, a taskmaster. Life is always pushing us, making us angry, making us late, irritating us; and, of course, we are always affected by the events of our lives.

When we do become conscious outside of time and space, it is said in the Work that we are "self-remembering." "Self-remembering" is letting the cares of the world become unimportant for even just one moment during the day. It is being lifted up and allowing yourself to realize that, although you are a tiny person on a very large globe in the middle of the gigantic universe, you are also a wonderful creation, and the Lord is with you, the heavens are around you, and you are a spiritual being. To remember that total reality and to push thoughts of everything material or natural out of your mind for a minute, or even one second, is to "remember" yourself. Of course, when you are first learning how to self-remember, you will fall back down again and check your watch—you're late!—and you fall back down to the natural line and into time and space again. But this temporary setback can be overcome with practice, so that self-remembering can last longer as you progress in the Work.

To understand self-remembering, you have to do it. One way is to remember someone you love. When there is someone you love and are very close to, whether a spouse, a friend, or a child, you may take them for granted. However, if you have ever been in a mall and lost a child, you suddenly remember how much you love that child. Another example of suddenly remembering is when someone dies. The day before the death you may have taken that person for granted. You may have forgotten how much you loved him or her. But the love is still there and can suddenly be remembered. If you lost someone and then woke up in the morning and the person was suddenly present again, you would remember your love and shower them with it. On an ordinary day, it may take a certain effort or energy to bring love to awareness, and self-remembering also has that quality. However, to the degree that you self-remember and rise above time and space, to that degree you will actually feel time and space stop.

Usually, we are not self-remembering. In fact, when we interact with other people, usually we do not experience each other; we experience our collective reactions to each other. That is true even with our most loved ones. We look at them, we have thoughts, we have memories, we have reactions. It is a rare event when we look at someone and our mind is quiet enough to get that little jolt of seeing them as they really are. And even when that does happen, we usually go back immediately into our typical reaction.

In the Work this is called "recurrence" when every day is just a mindless repetition of former moods. Life becomes so repetitious we think things like, "Oh, it's Monday again. . ." Well, it's not the same Monday; there's no circle to eternity. It's only because we tell ourselves it's Monday *again* that our Monday is the same old Monday.

Of course, we can Work on our recurring negative responses to certain people or situations. Before we Work, we are totally identified with that kind of behavior, seeing people and circumstances through our memories of the past. We don't even notice what the price of doing that is.

When we first Work on "recurrence" in our life, even if we don't do it well, we nonetheless get an awakening to the nature of this state of sleep, this mechanical way of living and reacting. Then it occurs to us that "recurrence" is costing a price, sometimes a very high price in your life.

When we awaken to this realization, we see the Work in a different way. We look at our life and see the sins involved, which are those kinds of memories and feelings that are not appropriate for the situation. And if we say "No!" to them, we will really know what it is costing us to respond automatically. We see how recurrence limits our thoughts, feelings, and actions.

Memories also limit our experience when we compare new experiences to them. EST philosophy describes how we put certain experiences in a little silver box, metaphorically speaking. Perhaps we compare every other experience to a special experience we have put in the little silver box on our mantelpiece. Often a new experience does not quite measure up to the one in the box.

If we had a full experience without associations, it would beat any memory we may have of the past. But we are asleep right now! We have no concept of how much we miss. The sleep we are in is not allegorical; it is a real, spiritual sleep, and our memories are some of the things that hold us back from waking up.

New influences cannot enter when our minds are constantly telling us how we should think and feel. This is why the Work says we must give up our personal histories, in a sense, if we are going to make real progress.

Fear of the Future

Our fears can limit our experience just as our memories can.

Picture two people standing on the side of a hill. In a field below, there are flowers and butterflies. One of the two people feels "safe" because he wears the medieval kind of armor from head to toe, although he doesn't have anything to fear. The other person is running around in just a loin cloth, but he does have five little stones in a little leather pouch by his side. That's all he needs; should Goliath come, he is ready.

We don't need all the armor that we think we need. The love of self and pride in our own intelligence are big burdens that we carry around for protection against things that are never going to happen. Then we find we spend a lot of time out in the field unable to walk because of our armor, hardly able to move or be honest with each other because we are afraid. Relationships stop; they become very stagnant because they can't move with all that fear present.

A willingness to drop the armor and trust the Lord is important. We don't need the armor to go fight Goliath. Why are we afraid? The Lord said he is with us. But we say, "I'll take my armor just in case." There is a lot of that in us.

So both our worry about the future and our memories of the past keep us asleep. Being here now is a difficult thing to do because the past and the future keep us hypnotized so that we seldom have a full experience.

Still, our abilities for remembering and anticipating can be important and useful. We may be driving down the road and anticipate a curve. We may anticipate that it is slippery or icy and that may save our life! We may remember that when we drive in the snow the first time in the winter we should try the brakes to see how far we slide. So, for those things, we need anticipation, and we have the capacity for that anticipation and the memory for when we need it. They are important tools. However, the tail shouldn't wag the dog. Memories and anticipation are great except when they prevent us from experiencing the experience we are having, or could be having, right now, an experience that has no time and no space.

Unfortunately, what often happens is that the tail does wag the dog. We are driven by our anticipation. We anticipate winter and get concerned; we anticipate things that never will happen, which we nonetheless fear. We become driven by memory and anticipation, which are tools that should be useful to us, not hinder us.

For the inner person, there is no time and there is no space. The past is an appearance and so is the future. If we give up our conjectures about the future and memories of the past, we can have more happiness in the present.

Repentance Is the Beginning of Transformation

You should not despair when you look at your natural self, even though what you will see is often evil. If you *don't* see the evil within yourself, you are in real trouble! It is good if you do see the evil. Once you know that IT is not you, then the fact that you are seeing things in detail is the beginning of a very important process called repentance.

Nicoll views the important process of repentance as a transformation, a change of mind, a new way of thinking:

> John the Baptist . . . is portrayed as teaching *repentance*—that is, *metanoia* or change of mind, or transformation of thinking. Unless a person begins to think in some entirely new way he cannot enter upon all that follows in the teaching of Christ. . . .
>
> The real meaning of human life on earth is not to be found in external life, or in the things of life, but in the idea of a trans-formation which, happening within a man, leads to a state called the "Kingdom of Heaven." . . . It is this new idea, this change of mind, that is indicated by the word metanoia, which is so poorly and inadequately translated as repentance.[2]

Swedenborg outlined the elements involved in the process of repentance:

> [Repentance] cannot occur unless we know not only in general terms but also in detail that we are sinners. No one can know this except those who examine themselves and see the sins in themselves, and for that reason condemn themselves.
>
> — *True Christianity* §513

We should condemn the parts of ourselves that have evil present. Making evil our own will condemn us. However,

---

2. Maurice Nicoll, *The Mark* (Boston and London: Shambhala, 1985), 102, 104.

separation from evil is possible, if we are willing. Swedenborg explains how we can repent:

> True repentance means not only examining what we do in our lives, but also what we intend in our hearts. . . . We can examine what we intend in our hearts by examining our thoughts, for intentions show up in these. . . . If we do this repeatedly, we find the pleasures we get from those evils become with repetition unpleasant to us, and we end by consigning them to hell. This is what is meant by the Lord's words: "If you want to find your soul, you will lose it, and if you lose your soul for my sake, you will find it" (Matthew 10:39). Those who rid themselves of the evils in their heart by this kind of repentance are like people who at the right time uproot from their field the tares sown by the devil, so that the seeds planted by the Lord God the Savior find the ground unencumbered and grow into a crop (Matthew 13:24–30).
>
> — *True Christianity* §532

Change is a capability within us, but change does not happen immediately. Self-observation is the first process by which we begin to repent and then be freed. Only through self-observation are we able to see that IT is active a lot of the time and that what IT believes to be true is often false and what IT feels as good is often evil.

Here's an example of how IT thinks in wrong ways. Suppose that your child left a chore undone at home, and you got angry and snapped at him about his failure to live up to his responsibilities. A negative thought may insist, "This is really about training my child." The negative takes on a form that is believable to you. In this instance, a selfish love takes on the form of concern for your child. It is not a good love, and it is not true.

IT gets frustrated, but conscious effort and attention can lead you to say to yourself, "I just want to go with IT and embrace the anger (or other negative emotion), but what is going on spiritually?" You ask that question and you start to bring together the Work ideas and doctrine that you have studied, those things you have learned from higher influences. You look from that higher point of view—from those truths in your rational mind (above your natural mind)—and those truths enlighten you. And then the truths that you have gathered together attract goodness. You start to see the good of those teachings or truths that benefit this earth by changing or transforming the way you approach things in life. Then you are really raising yourself up. You are opening yourself to influences that can transform or change the way you operate in life, influences that change the affections that operate through you.

The Lord is bringing together our Work I's. He does this through the examinations of self that we do with our tasks, through the efforts we make to repent. There will be a time when we become upset, and suddenly Work I's help us. Our conscience will have enough power by then to stop the direction of our upset, and at that point our new will is active. We can't anticipate exactly when this happens for each of us, but perhaps we get little touches of it, little examples of what it could be like. That is what we are working toward—awakening more and more, so that a new will, and an eagerness to Work, grows within us.

Since awakening to your spiritual side is gradual, you may not notice big changes all at once. More likely, you will sense small changes, a brief realization that you shouldn't react in your regular manner. Such a realization can come in unexpected ways.

Earlier I used the example of a child not doing an assigned chore. Suppose that your child leaves a chore undone at home, and you recognize that you want to get angry, but you try to Work instead. Suppose that, instead of snapping at your child, you just sensed your hand. That was all you could do. If sensing your hand is all you can do, and you do it, you are taking a step you are capable of taking at this point in the process, and that is very important. So when you are in a negative state, instead of asking yourself "What's my ultimate spiritual goal?" and thinking generally about spiritual growth, ask yourself "What can I do right now?"

The process is like learning a difficult dive, a gainer three and a half. You can admit to yourself, "I can't do that yet, but I certainly can practice my approach, hurdle, and takeoff again. I can practice till I get better at these than they are now." The gainer three and a half may be four years down the road, but by working on the little steps, you are moving forward toward that day. When Working, the answer may be "sensing," or "stopping thought," or praying. If you become better at the small, early steps, the next time a negative comes, you will be able to do a little more.

You may say, "But if I concentrate on my hand by sensing, my children will be sneaking out the door without doing their chores!" It is better that your children sneak out the door than that a negative spends fifteen minutes with them through your anger or other negative emotion. It is better that your children don't get disciplined by a negative pretending to be teaching them and that you sit there looking at your hand. A negative will *not* teach your children about doing chores around the house. A negative *will* teach your children about what adults do, and that it is okay to be angry, to yell and holler, etc.

You don't get good fruit from bad trees; that is guaranteed. Negatives have no interest whatsoever in doing anything good for anybody. They only have interest in doing evil to people and relationships, especially to innocent and good relationships like marriage and family.

But remember, we are not talking about things on the natural plane. Your children should still clean up and do their chores. But it might shock them to have you stop once and look at your hand instead of getting angry. That will get their attention.

The Task for Chapter 7

This task is a great one for holidays as well as regular days. It is to see people and go to events without any memory of the past and without any thoughts of the future. Try to come to experiences brand new, like a little child. Come to experiences without all your old or usual reactions in the way. Come to events sort of wide-eyed, even when you are with people you think you know. Step out of your past, which is tainted with your subjective reactions. Come to the world in a new way. Experience every event directly the way it is.

This task is an effort to awaken. The following quote from Emanuel Swedenborg gives us good reason to try it: "Predictions about the future and memories of the past are what take away all pleasure and happiness in life" (*Spiritual Experiences* §2190).

The point of this task is to not have any "silver box" of memories on your mantelpiece this time. Do not have anything in your memory about an event before it happens. Experience each event as it is, to its fullest. Your experience may outdo anything you ever had in the past. And it may outdo anything you are ever going to have in the future, but next time it will not matter because you can let it go and again you will have a new experience.

CHAPTER 8
Space for a Spiritual Life

Change of attitude changes the way life touches you.
— *P.D. Ouspensky*

The Work is about making choices, about distinguishing one state of mind from another, one type of I within yourself from another type of I. Some states are good, some are bad, and some are neutral.

If you were given a pot of ball bearings and told that some of them were silver and some were steel, you might have a hard time distinguishing one type from another. However, if you had a magnet, you would not have a problem telling them apart.

The Work talks about a center within you that is like a magnet; this center has an affection for truth. That affection searches for the truth in religious teachings or divine revelation. A person has what the Work calls "magnetic center" if he or she has an affection for truth, especially for the kind of truth that can transform or change him or her to being more spiritual. We are searching for that kind of religion or truth. We are searching for states that can elevate us.

Of course, we are capable of turning away from divine revelation to focus totally on the lowest, natural level of life, if we so choose. A person who does that long enough will close his or her mind to spiritual things. The Work says there are those who do not have an active magnetic center because it has become passive. Perhaps such people are interested solely in money, possessions, or reputation, and so they turn their mind away from higher influences.

We use self-observation in the process of searching, distinguishing, and separating from negative states. Observing I, or self-observation, operates in the rational mind and is capable of seeing truth.

Truth that is given by the Lord is that which allows us to distinguish between what is good and what is evil. At first, you may think it is easy to distinguish between good and evil, but from self-observation, you will find that it is not always easy. You need the magnet or desire and you also need Observing I. A lot of good affections can suddenly be turned to their opposites and wind up as selfish loves. Observing I, where the truth lives, can distinguish between the states in us that are useful and states that are not.

When we first Work, we find we have a natural mind, we have sensual delights that we are allowed to enjoy, but we are not to be driven by them. I can enjoy eating candy occasionally, but I'd better not eat candy all day long, every day! Those are two different states, the first an enjoyment of natural delights and the second a state of being driven, or overwhelmed, by those delights.

Magnetic center brings together those truths that can be used by the spiritual mind. When there are enough truths, Work I's not only observe our states and experiences, but begin to lead our lives. Instead of being dominated by IT in our natural minds, we can be led by the Work I's in our rational minds as we make our choices in daily life.

If we examine our negative states and when they occur, then we develop more and more choices in the activities in which we participate, whatever those activities are.

The Lord is Life

It is useful to be aware of magnetic center and of our choosing between one state and another state. We also know that part of our choosing involves not identifying with undesirable states such as anger and anxiety. With Work, we can see that some of our experiences (negative states) are not us. They are just I's we may temporarily have with us. Maurice Nicoll wrote that, once we stop indulging in our negative I's, they begin to diminish. Our strength then goes from IT to a new personality.[1]

According to Swedenborg, although it feels as though we have the power to act ourselves, this power or ability to act actually comes from the Lord. Further, Swedenborg explained that it is important for us to acknowledge that all power to do comes from the Lord. There is a huge difference, spiritually, between experiencing your life from the Lord as if it is your own and living your life believing that it is your own.

The Lord is life. It is possible to turn your life over to him, trusting that he will take care of it. If you do this, you can enter the peace of real faith:

> [T]he only approach to further inner development is through humility, through the real experience, constantly renewed, that one *does not know* in fact, that one knows nothing but is always pretending to know.[2]

The appearance is that a person with magnetic center is searching for something, but in actuality it is the Lord, within the person's affection for truth who is doing the searching. A distinguishing is going on, and the Lord is searching for what is *his* in a person. He looks for those things that he has planted in a person with whom he can have a conjunction. The Lord is

---

1. Nicoll, *Commentaries*, 940.
2. Nicoll, *Commentaries*, 936.

searching, and he is going to find what he is looking for when we cooperate. Divine providence is constantly leading toward conjunction.

In the quote below from Ezekiel, the Lord says he is going to separate "between sheep and sheep" and bring his sheep together and take them to a place where they can feed on good food. The Work says there are mainly three types of food: "A" influences that are natural (not spiritual) food; "B" influences that are esoteric ideas and are good food, spiritually speaking; and "C" influences from divine revelation that are the best spiritual food. As we read this passage, we might think of the process of how magnetic center brings together our Work I's, which can in turn help us make better choices in daily life:

> For thus says the Lord GOD: I myself will search for my sheep, and will seek them out. As shepherds seek out their flocks when they are among their scattered sheep, so I will seek out my sheep. I will rescue them from all the places to which they have been scattered on a day of clouds and thick darkness. I will bring them out from the peoples and gather them from the countries, and will bring them into their own land; and I will feed them on the mountains of Israel, by the watercourses, and in all the inhabited parts of the land. I will feed them with good pasture, and the mountain heights of Israel shall be their pasture; there they shall lie down in good grazing land, and they shall feed on rich pasture on the mountains of Israel. I myself will be the shepherd of my sheep, and I will make them lie down, says the Lord GOD. I will seek the lost, and I will bring back the strayed, and I will bind up the injured, and I will strengthen the weak, but the fat and the strong I will destroy. I will feed them with justice . . . . I will save my flock, and they shall no longer be ravaged; and I will judge between sheep and sheep. . . . I will make with them a covenant of peace and banish wild animals from the land, so that they may live in the wild and sleep in the woods securely.
>
> — Ezekiel 34:11–16, 22, 25

Our Required Spiritual Alertness

So the Lord distinguishes between our states with regard to our intentions. Still, it is our job as human beings to distinguish between Work I's and the potentially harmful and selfish (or evil) states of mind we are all inclined to. Let me explain this with an analogy.

There is nothing wrong with nature or with our participating in, and even enjoying, natural or worldly activities. For example, there is nothing wrong with taking a leisurely walk through a beautiful field or through a forest. We can walk through the woods and relax. We can daydream or just walk and not think or worry about anything. We can find a little pond in the summertime and lie by the pond with our eyes closed and even take a nap. We might want to walk down by the beach, walk over the dunes and enjoy the warm sand under our feet and the wind blowing through the grass. There would be nothing wrong with that, would there? If someone said, "You'd better watch it! You'd better not relax!" you would wonder what his problem was. So having a relaxed attitude about our natural lives is all right under certain conditions.

But under other conditions a relaxed attitude can be dangerous. My wife and I were in North Carolina enjoying a pond one day when some people came by and asked if we were from around there. We said, "No. Why do you ask?" They knew by the way we were just enjoying ourselves that we were not from around there, because what we'd thought was a nearby log was actually a crocodile! In certain places and situations dangerous animals use camouflage in order to fit into the environment perfectly. People who live in certain places walk a little differently than we do, more aware. In North Carolina, people never even swim in those little ponds without taking a good look first; they stay more awake than my wife and I did. The locals can tell when there is a predator in the woods. They don't wait until they bump into it. When the crickets stop chirping and the birds stop singing, they know there is something in the woods on the ready.

Spiritually, we must stay alert, when one of our selfish loves begins to stir. If we are asleep, or only half awake, we first become aware of dangerous animals only when they attack us! The Bible says *Awake* (Isaiah 52:1) and to be watchful (Luke 21:36). The thief comes when you least expect it.

There is nothing wrong with our living our natural life, in time and space, with our natural needs such as a job and a home, trying to get the car fixed and all that. But be careful! The natural level of the mind contains spiritually neutral thoughts, feelings, and experiences, but it also contains IT, and IT's negative, selfish states. We can be attacked spiritually at the natural level in a way we simply cannot be attacked in higher levels of our minds, the rational and spiritual levels.

What does this mean, in a practical sense? It means that you should try to see things from a Work point of view *before* your selfish loves become active. Once your will has become active, you are having a temptation, and that is when you will have trouble dragging a wild beast off your arm, spiritually speaking. It is very difficult, but if you become aware that trouble is going to attack you, then watch it!

Zen philosophy talks about people who have done the Work as being "watchful like men crossing a winter stream." They are alert like someone aware of danger. We are in a dangerous world, not because this world is dangerous but because we live in the spiritual world right now. We have to be careful.

We can be aware of warning signs of impending danger, such as a snake in a sand dune. I'm not going to try to convince you that these dangers exist; I'm just going to mention some words.

We call the first warning *likes and dislikes.* The Work tells us that likes and dislikes are not just part of the natural world. They are predators sitting in IT. When they become active, when you dislike something, underneath that disliking is often contempt for someone. Under contempt is often anger. Under anger is fury. This predator may just growl, or then again, it may take a swipe at your face or jump on you. You never know.

Another warning sign is the *urge for change*. The affection that has the urge for change is a bodily affection. Things are going along with no problem, then suddenly there is *the urge for change*. It may create impatience or irritation, and it might just bite you or your family. Sometimes it happens when you pull up to a red light. You could have made it across except that other guy in front of you decided to obey the law. Even that situation is the urge for change. There are many. Just be aware of whenever you do not want things the way they are, when you want things different from how they are right that minute. That is the urge for change.

Time and space are also to be noticed. I was watching a football game on television recently. Actually I was watching two shows; I was watching the football game and I was watching my natural mind watching the football game. My natural mind was furious, frustrated, and discontent. I asked myself, "Does this negative state have to do with time?" My answer was, "No, I don't care what time it is." Space? Well, yes, that was the answer. If I lived in another city and was rooting for the other team, I would be happy! For a second I pretended I did live there, and sure enough, my natural mind became pleased. IT's an idiot!

At a different time, I was watching a football game involving two cities I have no strong connection to, and I could really enjoy it because I did not care who won. But then my son asked, "Whom should we root for? Mother was born in Michigan, and we have relatives in San Francisco." Of course we could identify with either one of the teams and be happy when that team won, but the problem was we would be sad when that team lost if the goal was to dominate and have our side win!

Situations far more serious than this one come around often, and you can watch out for them if you stay aware.

Everything that we presently are, we have to give up. That is why the Bible says that we must be born again (John 3:3). Unless we are raised up from the natural mind to the rational or spiritual mind and give up those things of the natural world belonging to time and space, we cannot become spiritual.

The Lord wants us to give up being angry at the referee who says it is not a first down. Your anger is like a snake living in you. If you live in Philadelphia you may prefer the Eagles, although you do not even know an Eagle team member, never had a conversation with one, and the truth is, there may be more members from Philadelphia on the opposing team than there are on the Eagle team! All you really want is something you can identify with in some way and then like or dislike the other team because of it. If you stay in that kind of attitude, you are going to get bitten a lot. You are going to get angry.

However, there is a state above that attitude where we can be spiritual. We are created to be spiritual. It is true that, if we become more spiritual, our friends may think we are becoming boring. Perhaps we're not gossiping with friends as much as we used to or not driving as fast or beeping our horn as often as we used to. That is why the Work refers to our living according to higher principles (even if it displeases others) as "giving up your life." The Work is about changing, and we cannot change while staying the same.

You may think, *You are asking me to give up everything I care about!* You may believe that, if you give up a negative emotion, you will have nothing. But what you would give up is as nothing compared to what you would get if you gave up your selfish inclinations.

Of course, it is very difficult to give up our life as we have come to know it. One reason is that we are already established in what the Work calls our "level of being." Most of us are operating at a lower, natural level of being and are unaware of the effects of that. If we live at a lower level, then we attract— perhaps even invite—actions that are based on our emotional, self-destructive level.

Let's say that you are at a stop sign, and you get angry at another driver. You may say it is infuriating when someone stops in front of you like that, but your level of being has attracted that experience. It looked like the event just happened that way, but the truth is that you attracted the experience. Like a magnet, our anger and frustration will seek out situations that will fulfill their needs. Once we start changing the kind of person we are and begin to elevate ourselves to a higher level, then our outer problems will upset us less.

The Work states that we cannot change life and that we cannot change other people. We can, however, change ourselves. We opened this chapter with a quote from P.D. Ouspensky: "Change of attitude changes the way life touches you."[3] As has been stressed throughout this book, we must become aware of our level of being, our current state, and examine it to see how we can lift ourselves above the unimportant, everyday situation and concentrate on the spiritual and the eternal.

Maurice Nicoll explained how self-observation serves us in our quest for a higher spiritual state. He describes a space between an external world event, or "impression," and our reaction to it.

> Self-observation opens a little room, a little space, and time, between the incoming impression and its lodgement in the place that habitually receives it and reacts to it. Self-observation begins to make an inner life in a man. Eventually he under-goes a growth of Consciousness in this way—namely, that Consciousness begins to intervene between the impression and the reaction.[4]

When we Work, we try to create a space for consciousness. We try to wake up, and we do that with self-observation.

After we have woken up a bit, or made a space for consciousness, we want to expand that space. We want enough

3. Nicoll, Commentaries, 979.
4. Nicoll, Commentaries, 981.

room to receive our new state from above rather than from our usual lower, habitual way of perceiving things. When we give up an evil (such as a negative thought or habit), we give up what is false along with it, and a positive that is both good and true can then flow in.

We can expand a conscious space by bringing to mind ideas that come from higher influences. A higher influence could take the form of a formal religious teaching, such as "See, I am making all things new" (Revelation 21:5) or just a single true idea such as *truth from the Lord can transform me.* Bringing just one such powerful idea or truth to that conscious space will help it expand.

Gifts from the Lord

The Lord's providence is in the least of the least. He is not just providing for our lives in general ways. He is in the very least of every thought or happening, in every jot and tittle. His Word is divine—not only the Word but the very words used in it—and the Lord is within everything that happens.

This is an extremely powerful idea, and we can use it in our lives. It is easy to think of day-to-day examples. I was taking my son to a magic show, and on the way I took a wrong turn on a road that I thought would take me to the theater. Instead the road brought me out to a car dealership. How did that make me feel? How does IT feel when IT finds out IT took a wrong turn? IT's irritated. What could you bring to an event like this if it happened to you? The truth is that the least thing that the Lord allows in providence will be good for you, spiritually, and it will turn out for your eternal spiritual welfare. When I brought that thought from divine revelation to my experience arriving at the car dealership, I was immediately happy with things as they transpired.

I know that the Lord is within everything that happens, not just the small things. My taking the wrong turn is not a serious event. But what if I had been in a bus accident yesterday and had lost my left arm? Then my understanding of divine providence could really make a difference or change how I feel and how I react.

People who have had near-death-experiences have trust in providence. Even if what brought them the near-death experience was an accident that left their body permanently injured, the idea of providence sustains them and remains true for them. They actually see their situation in the light of that trust. Leon Rhodes writes of the near-death experience:

> We know that the Near Death Experience is said to be ineffable and that it is something that will not be forgotten. It has none of the qualities of a dream, hallucination or fantasy, and it has powerful aftereffects. Universally, NDErs report that they no longer have any fear of death, and nearly all experiencers declare that they believe in a life after death.[5]

Meister Eckhart, the thirteenth-century German mystic, of anyone I ever read, believed that everything that ever happened to him was a gift from the Lord. Whether appearing good or bad, he believed it was the best gift that the Lord could possibly give him, and he would not pray for anything to be any different. There can be no restlessness unless it comes from your self will. When you are thwarted it is your own attitude that is out of order.

> One person who has mastered life is better than a thousand persons who have mastered only the contents of books, but no one can get anything out of life without God. . . . Perfection depends only on accepting poverty, misery, hardship, disappointment, and whatever comes in course, and accepting it willingly, gladly, freely, eagerly until death, as if one were prepared for it and therefore unmoved by it and not asking why.[6]

5. Leon S. Rhodes, *Tunnel to Eternity: Swedenborgians Look Beyond the Near Death Experience* (Bryn Athyn, Pa.: n.p., 1996), 43.

6. Raymond B. Blakney, trans., *Meister Eckhart: A Modern Translation* (New York: Harper and Row, Publishers, Incorporated, 1941), 236.

Within providence, some events occur that are in the Lord's will, some events occur that are by his permission, and still other events are allowed to occur by his leave. He lets us live in freedom, allowing things to happen that he might not choose. Some things, especially horrendous things, he does not design but allows to happen in his mercy.

I think permission is *within* providence. It is not like providence is over here, and everything out of the Lord's control is over there in the "leave-or-permission" areas. Leave and permission are within providence and are the means by which providence handles the least details of a world where freedom of choice is allowed. A bad experience, like a drunk who comes home, vomits, and falls down, isn't something the Lord wills. But the Lord can use the experience, as he uses every experience, to benefit that person. There is a goodness within permission that the Lord gives us regardless of the appearance.

The Divine, in permission, is doing the best thing that can be done, from total wisdom and total love, within each event the Lord does not wish to occur but allows. He is there. Events are not out of his control. He hasn't lost touch with us. He is within every situation or state with us as part of the process. With every experience we have, whether we break an arm or lose a leg, we have to trust that he will take the experience and turn it to our best eternal welfare.

You may be asking, "What about when something bad happens to someone else? How am I supposed to react to that?" You can know that the event is the best thing for that person's eternal spiritual welfare. But knowing that need not take away from your feelings of sorrow, compassion, and pain that they have to go through such means in order for them to reach a certain spiritual level of well-being later on. If you take a five-year-old girl to the hospital and she has to have her stomach pumped, you know it is for her welfare. But still it hurts that such discomfort is the means by which she is helped. There is real suffering. Mutual love is good, and you don't want to get rid of it.

We must not use the Work as an excuse to become an unfeeling person. Objectivity is not coldness. A negative thought asks, "What kind of God would allow this?" Considering the event as productive to eternal welfare protects us from that hellish attitude.

Permission is within providence because people must be left in freedom. Freedom allows us to feel as if life is our own. It is useful to have to decide what is right and what is wrong, because it makes our life feel like ours, even though we need to acknowledge that it is not.

When people in freedom decide to do evil, then others have to contend with that evil. Permission is the means by which divine love and wisdom handle every detail of the choice some people make to be evil. It is not loss of control; it is within the Lord's control. It is better that we are allowed to do evil than that we be forced to do good.

The more conscious we become, the more we will feel empathy for other people. That will happen because we will be aware of things we were insensitive to beforehand. The feeling won't be anger that certain things happen; it will be sharing the other person's pain and longing to comfort them.

Nothing that happens is a mistake. The Lord is there.

Suppose you went to a dentist who said, "Look, I have to take out one of your teeth. I can't give you much novocaine since you are allergic to it, and the procedure is going to hurt, but trust me! You can relax. Don't worry, I am not going to make any mistakes. I know what I am doing."

Different people would have different responses. A person who does not trust the dentist would have a certain experience of sweat and struggle and pain. A person who totally trusted the dentist would relax, and although the procedure would still hurt, that person would have a very different experience than the person who does not trust.

Bad things happen, and the Lord himself said that while we are in the world we will have stress; he also said, "Take courage; I have conquered the world" (John 16:33).

I was given a pillow with a quote on it: *Serenity is not peace from the storm; it is peace within the storm.* The storm is our natural life. We are not going to do this Work and get away from all the trouble in life. The storm is still there, but the Work is where we can believe and know that, even while it storms, the Lord is still there. Trust in the Lord is something you will even feel in your body. If I make a wrong turn and wind up someplace I didn't intend to be, I don't have to be angry or miserable. The Lord is there. I can Work right there, wherever I find myself. The Lord didn't forget me.

The Lord is within permissions and within leave. He never chooses to have a child hurt, for example, but he is with every hurt child; and by believing that truth you have an entirely different feeling than if you think the Lord is not there or that the situation is out of his control. Someone called up a minister to ask the question, "How can all these horrible things happen?" The minister said, "You mean you are thinking about all the horrible things that *would* happen if the Lord wasn't taking care of us?" That same minister interviewed several people, asking what the best experiences of their lives were. They each told of a terrible experience from which they learned a lot and that changed their life. The Lord came to them through those horrendous experiences.

The Task for Chapter 8

Recall a spiritual truth when you are experiencing a negative state. In the Work, this is called "bringing the Work to an incoming impression." When life suddenly doesn't go the way you want it to, recall some truth rather than reacting negatively.

The Lord's providence is in the least things, and all events occur in order to lead us and give us gifts for our eternal spiritual welfare. Take such an idea and bring it to the interruptions in your life, to those things that don't go the way you want them to go.

If you can catch yourself before you step on a snake, spiritually speaking, if you can catch yourself before your will is active, and you then put truth into the space between the event and your reaction, you will be well. On the other hand, if you can't do this, and you find you are reacting, still bring a true thought down. Raise your eyes and look up to something higher, and although you may be bitten, you still are not going to die. You will learn from the experience.

CHAPTER 9
"Remembering" Ourselves

Sometimes this moment of self-observation will change you for the moment completely. A sufficient number of such Work moments may change you, not for a moment, but for all your life.

— *Maurice Nicoll*

*P*redatory beasts that hide in the environment are like certain negative states of being that hide in our natural minds.

Well, once I was attacked by a snow leopard! Returning from doing an errand, I was home by 9:20 PM, looking forward to a 9:30 television program. As I came in the door, my wife asked if I would pick up our youngest daughter from her dance lesson. As I turned around, I thought of the task: bring truth to an incoming impression or negative state. Yes, I thought, it's the perfect task. There are no interruptions. Everything is for the best. I felt pretty good about that instead of feeling resentful.

So, I went out to my car. A snow plow had snowed me in, but I thought I could back out fast and get over the pile of snow. My daughter was going to meet me outside of her dance studio, so I knew by now she was probably out there waiting in the cold. I couldn't scrape off the ice from my windshield, but I made a little hole in the ice allowing me to barely see through the windshield. When I got in the car, I tried to pull out fast, but I couldn't surmount the snow pile.

I was still thinking about the task and feeling that it was working pretty well because I still felt okay about things. So, I gunned the engine again, not aware that my wife had just taken all the trash out, putting glass on the top and cans in the middle. When I hit the trash can going at a fast speed, of course, the glass went everywhere.

At this point, the beast bit me. I put my hand brake on harder than usual and got out of the car. I slammed the car door shut. Since the broken glass was white, it could not be seen very well on the white snow. Having no gloves on for such a short trip, I picked up the glass I could see with my bare hands, knowing all the while that my daughter was still waiting for me out in the freezing cold. I got back into the car and backed up, trying to avoid the remaining glass, but wound up with my front wheels on the curb and my back wheels off the curb. I couldn't move the car at all.

By now my wife had heard some noise, and she came out. I was so "identified" that I kicked the tires and screamed, and tried to turn into the Hulk. I figured at any minute I could just pick the whole car up and walk with it.

Of course, right after that I tried to do the Work again, and perhaps I reduced the time I held on to the feeling of frustration. I definitely experienced the difference between Working and just thinking about the Work. As I was just thinking about the Work, I had a picture of myself going to get my daughter and doing everything nicely—the picture that IT came up with, a picture that could easily be destroyed.

For me, being attacked by a snow leopard was a meaningful experience because it underscored the fact that even a person committed to the Work can backslide. I still have to pay attention to what I am actually saying and doing, rather than just thinking about Working.

In *Worship and Love of God*, Emanuel Swedenborg discusses listening to what we say, which, of course, is part of self-observation:

> Our conversation makes it fairly clear how unruly a crowd our
> mind would hold if our ideas should break loose uninvited,
> since what we say flows from our mind. Our words advertise
> what our state of mind is—specifically, whether it is a vision
> of natural-world goals or of spiritual ones that motivates our
> actions. If a vision of merely natural-world goals does, it is a sign
> that those ideas have invaded the palace and hold the keys.
>
> — *Worship and Love of God* §66, footnote i

If we listen to what we say, we will find that it is usually
based on time and space. If we hear ourselves saying, "I came
home and got angry because dinner wasn't ready," we can see
that we are thinking on the natural level and that dinner's not
being ready appears to be, but is not, the cause of our anger.

If we listen to other people, we will find that the way they
talk reveals where they are spiritually. If we listen to ourselves,
we will notice the same thing. What we say does indicate
where we are.

Swedenborg also wrote about the different levels within our
minds and the fact that a lower level cannot work its way up
to a higher level:

> No organ of perception can understand what intelligence is; nor
> can intelligence, insofar as it is merely natural, understand
> what wisdom is. It is the higher that must be the judge of the
> lower. Therefore the lower exists by favor and help of the
> higher.
>
> — *The Economy of the Animal Kingdom*, Part 2, §266

So we cannot think our way to perception about spiritual
things. A lot of the Work is directed at stopping the activity of
a lower level of our minds so that we can become receptive to
higher levels. We cannot build our way to heaven or grow
spiritually without acknowledging the Lord's help.

When the Lord Can Become Active within Us

In literature such as the Work, the Tao, and especially Swedenborg's writings, we can read about the necessity of giving up, of letting go, of sacrificing, of dying, and of giving our lives over to the Lord. This is an important part of spiritual growth and yet the question arises, "What do we do?" The answer is that we cannot do by our own effort, and we are not to do, but we participate in some form in the process of spiritual growth as we struggle against evil:

> In the case of charity and faith, the Lord acts and the person acts in response to the Lord, for the Lord's activity lies within the person's passivity. Therefore the ability to act aright is from the Lord.   — *True Christian Religion* §576[2]

This quotation mentions "the Lord's activity within the person's passivity." From this, we can infer that we *allow* ourselves to be reformed. I think this is significant. A person cannot grow spiritually from his or her own intelligence or from his or her own active effort. In fact, we contribute nothing. However, if we become passive to trying to grow spiritually from ourselves and sacrifice that inclination to try, then something else in us can become active, not from ourselves but from the Lord. Then spiritual growth can begin from the Lord within our passive attitude of allowing him to do the Work for us.

If we die, we will be reborn. It appears as if spiritual growth is being done by us, but our role is to become passive, to give up self-intelligence, to give up self-power, to give up self-conceit, and to depend on the Lord as we resist evil. We have to let go of self in order to allow the Lord to become more active within us.

I found in teaching diving that I would much rather have someone come for lessons who knows nothing—and who knows he knows nothing—than have someone who thinks that he already knows how to dive. The latter is full of himself, thinking he already knows what it takes to dive successfully. It is hard for such a person to let himself be taught because he thinks he already has the answers.

The process of learning involves not knowing. Listen to the teacher as if you have never before heard what the teacher is saying, and then you will learn something. The Work asks you to become passive, to give up and let go.

We need to learn to trust divine providence, even in those times when we do not understand its workings:

> The only radical cure for anxiety is a spiritual trust in the Divine Providence. . . . [T]o the extent that men truly believe in Him and trust in His providence the Lord removes their anxieties.
>
> Yet the nature of that trust must be rightly understood. The Word nowhere promises that those who trust in the Divine Providence will be spared suffering, or even death. Indeed, in asking for their trust, the Lord warned His disciples: "In the world ye shall have tribulation." Yet He added: "But be of good cheer: I have overcome the world." The answer of [Swedenborg's] Writings . . . is that whatever befalls those who trust in the Divine Providence—whether good or ill, happy or unhappy—is yet conducive to their eternal welfare.[1]

Right now we may be full of our own thinking, full of our own opinions, full of our own likes and dislikes. So how do we adopt a passive attitude that will be useful? One way is to pray and ask the Lord for help when we are in a difficult situation. Another way is to think about divine providence and have trust in the Lord. Still another way to adopt a useful, passive attitude is to "stop thought," which asks that we stop thinking, not so that we do not have any intelligence, but are open to

---

1. W. Cairns Henderson, "Care for the Morrow," in *Selected Editorials by W. Cairns Henderson* (Bryn Athyn, Pa.: Academy of the New Church Press, 1978), 140–141.

the higher perception that will come in if our own thinking is
not in the way.

If you had a book by Confucius, written in Chinese, it
probably wouldn't be very useful in your life. Someone would
have to translate the book, so it could have meaning to you. In
some important ways, the Work and the writings of Emanuel
Swedenborg are similar to books by Confucius. In fact, that is
why I read Nicoll. He helps me translate Work ideas into my
daily life.

In order for divine revelation or the Work to have any
meaning in our life, we have to take what is said and translate
it into examples. Ask yourself, "What does that mean in my
life? How can I actually experience what they are talking
about? How would I actually know that it is happening or
taking place in my life?" Without this kind of personal
translation, we will not be putting the transformative ideas
to their best use.

Subjective Thinking

I keep bringing up "likes and dislikes" because they are a
prime example of subjective thinking, which is based upon
personal feelings. Subjective thinking is the opposite of
objective thinking, which considers facts without bias. Likes
and dislikes are symptoms of the way we live our lives
subjectively rather than objectively. Likes and dislikes are veils
that stand between other people and us.

Let's say that I am driving down the road and notice lawn
ornaments in someone's yard. Now, somewhere in my history I
was told that lawn ornaments are cheap and common, so when
I see other people's ornaments I don't like them. Even though I
have ornaments in my own pond and I like them, I dislike
other people's lawn ornaments. But now, because I am in the
Work, when I drive by other people's yards, I try to put my
dislike aside and think of what affection was active in the
person who put the lawn ornaments there. What is it that they

are trying to share? They obviously like the ornaments and are trying to share that love with me. If I am busy disliking the ornaments, I can't appreciate what the person is trying to share with me.

If you listed all of the things you like in food and put it against a list of all the foods in the world, your list would be very short in comparison. If I made a list of all the architectural styles that I like compared to all the styles that there are, my list wouldn't be very long. You can see that I limit my appreciation. I limit the amount of affection that people can share with me because I won't let anything in that does not already fit my likes.

We could say that this kind of thinking is subjective thinking, because it is based on me rather than on a broader reality. If we thought objectively rather than subjectively, we would be able to see the Lord and his love in everything in reality and fact. We would see ourselves objectively, too, including our negative states and the fact that the Lord forgives us. However, we seldom see our lives objectively, in the light of truth or reality.

Our subjective orientation is both personal and cultural or social. On the personal side are selfish loves and a self-serving point of view. Selfish loves stand between our experience of things as they are and our likes and dislikes. A thick cloud of selfish love and love of the world often hangs between us and other people.

On the cultural or social side are inheritance, upbringing, tradition, and social pressures. In different centuries and different places, people collectively have certain subjective blind spots. Subjective beliefs or values commonly held by any group of people do not seem odd at all to the people living at that time in that system, even though those beliefs or values may be very subjective and very far from objective reality.

Gurdjieff's little book *Beelzebub's Tales to His Grandson* portrays our world objectively, in story form. The book makes the point that, if we look at things from an objective point of view, we will see that our judgments are often subjective rather than objective.

One story has an alien coming into a bar during a football game. The alien, who has a very different belief system from our own, hears everybody in the bar yelling and screaming and declaring which team is best. The alien asks the people in the bar, "How do you determine which team is best? Do you study statistics, or do you interview the people on the teams, or do you look into the players' backgrounds?" He is told, "No, we take a mental tape measure from the tip of our nose to where the team practices, and if one team practices closer to us or to where we live, then that is considered the best team! Of course, there are a few exceptions. One is if a relative of ours plays on a different team, then that team is better. Another exception might be if we are betting a lot of money and really need to know which team is likely to win among all the teams."

In another part of Gurdjieff's book, Beelzebub, who had already visited our planet several times, now is coming one more time. Beelzebub's grandson keeps asking him about these beings or humans Beelzebub has talked about. The child says, "Tell me about these people who live in America, especially those in New York." So the grandfather tells him about the first time he visited the United States. Beelzebub tried to talk to the people in power, but no one would talk to him. So he went back to his starship, and the crew explained that the reason he was being ignored was that he did not have enough green things. They further explained that the green things were about two or three inches by five inches and that anyone would need to have some to be well thought of in America, especially in New York. The crew told Beelzebub, "If you go back there with enough of these green things, they will even get a camera crew and interview you and will want your opinion on many things."

If an alien being comes down to a post office that sells current stamps, and down the street there is another store that sells antique stamps, the alien might go to the first place to buy a stamp. Finding he needs more stamps to mail something, he might go to the second store. There he would be told, "Oh, you can't mail anything with these stamps, they are old, and anyway, they cost $2,500." The alien would ask why an old stamp costs so much if it can't even be used to mail a letter. He might be told that a stamp with a mistake on it, like having the picture upside down or crooked, is worth even more. He would say, "You mean if it's older and has a mistake and you can't use it, it costs the most?" He would be puzzled indeed!

If the alien went to the stock exchange, he would be really shocked. On the alien's planet, people learn about a business; and if they think it is a good company, product, or service, they decide to invest in it. But here it doesn't matter what service or what product is offered; the only thing many people want to know is whether the company's stock will sell for more tomorrow than it does today. We measure how much a stock is worth not only by looking at the company, but by guessing how much people will pay for the stock in the future!

If the alien went to an art dealer like Sotheby's and someone who had not even looked at a painting still in a crate bid $54 million on it, the alien might be amazed. The alien might have just walked by some artists in the park who could not sell any, even though their paintings were very good. The alien asks the buyer, "How could you buy a painting in a crate for $54 million?" He is told, "Because I believe that next year someone will offer me even more money for it." So the purchase was made solely for the purpose of making money in the future. In addition, money isn't being used to buy art—art is used to buy money! That is subjective. An objective point of view would consider how much the buyer appreciates the art piece at the present time as the means of determining its worth, not how much he thinks someone else will be willing to pay for it next year.

The stories about the alien tell us a little about objective and subjective consciousness, and objective and subjective values. Is it important? Yes, it is.

With regard to attitudes about money, I believe that we were all born for something higher than to make money. If we make money in the pursuit of a higher goal, that is fine; but if money is the sole goal of anything we do, then that is a subjective goal.

With regard to our attitudes toward other people and the types of activities we participate in, I personally don't think bull fights would take place if everyone were objectively conscious, but that is just my opinion. I definitely don't think the Holocaust would have taken place if people had been objectively conscious.

When we see the reality of each human being's worth, we can't be part of violence, whatever form that might take, physical, verbal, or otherwise. Many actions that take place in our families and between us and others in the world would be totally impossible if we reached objective consciousness and saw things as they really are.

Self-Remembering

One of the steps toward objective thinking is to engage in self-remembering. What is self-remembering? It says in the Work that you should "remember yourself" once a day; and if you can't do it once a day, then do it twice a day! One way to self-remember is to focus on and keep your goal or effort to grow spiritually. In earlier chapters, I described other ways to self-remember. We remember ourselves when we are awakening spiritually, when we pull ourselves away from being identified with negative emotions, when we become conscious outside of time and space, when we let the cares of the world become unimportant to us for even one moment, when we feel aware that we are spiritual beings, or when we remember the love we have for someone.

To remember yourself is to be conscious simultaneously in three different ways at one time. First, you are to be aware of the external world. Second, simultaneously you are to be aware of your responses, your reactions in thoughts, emotions, and sensations. Third, at the same time as you do the first two things, you become aware of your own presence and having a sense of "I am," which enables you to become aware of yourself doing the first two steps. Self-remembering is looking down from a higher place on your own responses to something happening in the world.

You may be aware of being where you are, of *being here now.* You know how it feels to be here, right? Still, although you are on the globe as a tiny speck in the universe, the Lord is with you, and you can remind yourself, "I am here." Just for a second, feel your existence, with the feeling of "I am." Is there a change in your awareness?

Becoming aware of all your senses, one by one, can help you to self-remember. First, become aware of only your sense of sight. Notice the colors in the room or the color of your clothes. Then add your sense of hearing by listening to any sounds around you, still aware of what you see. Notice any scent in the air and any taste in your mouth. Then add your sense of touch to the others by noticing the texture of whatever you are touching. And last, add the feeling of your own presence or being and feel or experience a sense of "I am."

Self-remembering is not a thinking experience. The "I am" is not IT. The "I am" is awareness of the wonder of your existence. You can be aware of your actual size in God's great universe. You can be aware of being a human being physically and spiritually, of being a miracle of God's creation. Self-remembering is an effort to wake up and have a different awareness, a different consciousness. Self-remembering is an increase of awareness as to our actual existence, not only naturally but spiritually.

You will find yourself unusually aware and changed by this type of self-remembering.

Self-Remembering and Objective Thinking

You may have watched people walking down the street, all inside themselves, in their heads, talking to themselves. If they were instead remembering themselves, they would see, they would hear, they would feel, they would smell, they would taste. They would be conscious and aware. If they were remembering themselves they would experience "I am."
    Concerning this, Gurdjieff said:

> A man must begin by realizing what he actually is now. He is not yet conscious. When he sees this, he must begin by remembering himself. If a man could remember himself he would be at a higher level of consciousness. He would be no longer asleep. As a result, many illusions would fall away from him and everything would appear in a new light. If he went on he would reach a state of consciousness above that of Self-Remembering—the state of Objective Consciousness. In that state he would see things as they really are.[2]

And Nicoll wrote:

> Have you lifted yourself even once to-day out of your mechanical moods? Even an act of noticing a negative state, of observing that you are negative or speaking negatively, separates you a little. Sometimes this moment of self-observation will change you for the moment completely. A sufficient number of such Work-moments may change you, not for a moment, but for all your life.[3]

Our temporary subjective point of view is a necessary phase on our individual journey to more heavenly states. But we need to try to wake up and see the truth.

---

2. Nicoll, *Commentaries*, 1003.
3. Nicoll, *Commentaries*, 1005.

The very act of self-remembering—whether we do it by realizing what a tiny speck in the universe we are, or by recognizing the incredible wonder we are just being (as a creation of God)—the act of self-remembering helps us become more objective and less subjective.

>∈

The Task for Chapter 9

Your task will be to remember yourself "if not once a day, then twice a day."

When do you remember yourself? Whenever it occurs to you, or at a set time, if you are a routine-type person. Here's a reminder: whenever a negative state occurs, that would be a good time to remember yourself. Here's another reminder: any time you become aware of making a negative remark or innuendo about another person, you would be wise to remember yourself. You can use self-remembering to separate from negative emotions.

I don't recommend overdoing it. Don't try self-remembering for half an hour at a time. Just try it for a minute, maybe two minutes. Then let it go.

But practice is important. The Work says that if you practice remembering yourself, you have an excellent chance of remembering to do it when a strong negative state hits. Then you will get a lot out of it.

In his work *In Search of the Miraculous*, Ouspensky describes what it felt like to experience self-remembering on a street he knew well but which he suddenly saw anew. We too can practice self-remembering, and a time will come when we will be given a real experience of what it actually is. When the experience comes, you will know!

So raise your consciousness of "I am." Raise your awareness. Notice the states that interfere with your doing the task. Lift yourself out of your self, out of IT.

CHAPTER 10
Loving and Understanding the Neighbor

All real love is consciousness of another person's difficulties
through finding the same difficulties in yourself.

— *Maurice Nicoll*

We have been given two great commandments: to love
the Lord and to love the neighbor. The Lord creates us
with the built-in potential to love others. We are commanded
to love, and everything we feel, think, or do, is based on that.

The commandment to love is given all through the Bible. In
John 13:34–35, the Lord says:

> I give you a new commandment, that you love one another. Just
> as I have loved you, you also should love one another. By this
> everyone will know that you are my disciples, if you have love
> for one another.

When Jesus says, "*By this everyone will know that you are my
disciples, if you have love for one another,*" we can know that
those states within us that are capable of loving another person
are like the Lord's disciples. That is how we will know which
I's are Work I's. The I's to cultivate are those that are capable
of loving others. We can certainly distinguish those I's from
the states in us that cannot love other people.

We have the ability to love the Lord and the neighbor if we are willing to give up selfish loves—in other words, if we are Working.

Love and Charity

Loving the neighbor is a big experience, and it is a long road to loving the neighbor in actuality. We may go through different stages while trying to live that commandment. For example, we might begin by asking, "How am I to love? And how am I to love neighbors who do bad deeds?"

We'll discuss these issues more later in this chapter. For now, we can think of love as something that goes out from you toward someone else, something that wishes the best for that person, whoever they are.

In Swedenborg's theology, the concept of love is closely related to the idea of charity. Charity is a broad concept that involves much more than giving to the truly needy. Charity entails actually loving the neighbor, being useful, and using justice in our dealings with others.

> Charity is our spiritual life. . . . To love our neighbor is to do what is good, fair, and right in every deed and in every job. . . . So charity toward the neighbor includes each and every thing we think, will, and do. . . . Doing what is good and true is loving our neighbor.
> — *New Jerusalem and Its Heavenly Doctrine* §106

Another question we might ask is, "Who is my neighbor?" Swedenborg provides the answer:

> People believe that a sibling, relative, or other connection is more their neighbor than a stranger; and a fellow citizen more than a foreigner. But everyone is our neighbor according to his or her virtue.   — *Charity* §75

The soul of every man and woman is with the Lord. There is always some good in every person while he or she is on earth. So, everybody is our neighbor, in a sense, under all circumstances, no matter what, all the time. Every other human body is our neighbor, and we are to love them, even our enemies. The Lord tells us:

> "You have heard that it was said, 'You shall love your neighbor and hate your enemy.' But I say to you, Love your enemies and pray for those who persecute you...."   —Matthew 5: 43–44

> "But I say to you that listen, Love your enemies, do good to those who hate you, bless those who curse you, pray for those who abuse you."   —Luke 6:27–28

We can obey the commandment to love the neighbor by having good intentions toward everyone, considering everyone to be our neighbor.

So everyone is your neighbor in one sense. Yet in another sense they are not. We are to love the good in others, but not the evil. Swedenborg explains how we should differentiate:

> Those who love their neighbor with real charity inquire into others' characters and benefit them in different ways, depending on their type and degree of virtue.   —Charity §52

We must distinguish between when to do good to a certain neighbor and when not to do good to them. We should not do good indiscriminately, because doing that is not good.

For example, if you are an enabler, you are not helping the person enabled. If a drunk comes down the street and you give him a dollar to buy a drink, have you done him good? No. You are helping him do evil. You are helping to enslave him. You are doing evil to the good in him. Again, we hear the words of Swedenborg:

> For unless people have a right understanding of who the
> neighbor is, they will exercise charity uniformly and indis-
> criminately, toward the good and evil equally, as a result of
> which charity ceases to be charity. For with the benefits
> conferred on them the wicked harm their neighbor, whereas
> the good benefit theirs.   — Secrets of Heaven §6703

Swedenborg makes the connection between loving the neighbor and loving the Lord:

> Good itself is the neighbor. . . . Consequently, those governed
> by good are the neighbor, and they are the neighbor in the
> measure that good governs them. . . . Good is therefore the
> neighbor because the Lord is present in it. . . . Accordingly,
> when good is loved, the Lord is loved.
> — Secrets of Heaven §3768[2]

So, if we love the good in the neighbor, we love the Lord.

A Paradox

The Lord said, "Do not judge, so that you may not be judged" (Matthew 7:1). We cannot judge others because we cannot tell the difference between good and evil motives (or intentions) in other people. We can only see their behavior.

A person who is arrogant and contemptuous at the beginning of his life often regrets it and changes as he gets older and starts to grow spiritually. Although he becomes humble, his rough external may cling to him. So although he is now fifty years old and much mellower and very humble, he may still walk with his old swagger and have many of his old mannerisms. If you talk to him for ten minutes, you may penetrate this exterior, but it is still a lesson to us that you cannot judge from the external what a person is like on the inside.

We have difficulty distinguishing good from evil in other people because each of us has IT. If something is in agreement

with us or we love it, or it even looks like us, we may think it
is good because IT thinks it is good. IT thinks that anything
that favors IT is good and anything that does not favor IT is
evil. The Lord alone can actually see and judge the neighbor,
because he alone can see the good and bad clearly in that person.

So how are we to love the good in the neighbor when
we can only see their behavior and not their motives or
intentions? Swedenborg's response is simple: "Since . . . a
person's inner self . . . rarely reveals itself in the world, it is
enough for us to love our neighbor at the level on which we
do know her or him" (*True Christianity* §410[3]).

The Bible tells us that, in order to love good in the
neighbor, we must first make a search in ourselves and find
out what is good in ourselves from the Lord and what is evil
and selfish love. Jesus asked, "Why do you see the speck in
your neighbor's eye, but do not notice the log in your own
eye?" (Matthew 7:3) It is just an appearance that we can love
the neighbor before we give up selfish love. That appearance is
due to our favoring what is advantageous to us in the neighbor,
or liking something similar to us in him or her. Only after we
have cleansed ourselves will we be able to see more clearly
what is good in the neighbor and what is evil.

In addition to finding what is good and evil within
ourselves, we must separate from the parts of ourselves that
are not from the Lord. The Work, as we know, calls this
process "non-identification."

We can make a division in ourselves and see evils there
that formerly we could only see in our neighbor. If we search
for, find, and become separate from the evil in ourselves, then
something can be reborn in us. Eventually we can live in the
higher, spiritual part of ourselves, where the Lord is, and that
part will be able to perceive the good in the neighbor. That
part of us will also see what is not good in the neighbor, but
it will do so from love. Since the Lord loves everyone and
forgives everyone constantly, this process of making a division
in ourselves and living in the spiritual part will allow us to see
the good in people rather than condemn them.

The state we are in determines how truly we can love the neighbor. If we find that we have not made any division between good and evil in ourselves—if we feel like the evils with us are our own, and when we are angry, we think we *are* the anger—then we are probably still at a level in which we need to obey the simple rule to love the neighbor, any neighbor.

However, when we start to get a division and know that we are not our evil, even though there are evils with us, we are at a higher level. That which is good in us may be able to perceive that the neighbor is not *his* or *her* evil either, and we will feel good about our neighbor, in spite of the fact that he or she has evils, just as we all do. Of course, external considering and finding evils in ourselves will help a great deal in this Work.

Swedenborg explains that, at some point in our spiritual renewal, we will be able to distinguish between the good and the bad as if by second nature:

> At length, when [people] are regenerate, they do not do good to any but the virtuous and godly, for at this point they are stirred not simply by an affection for the person they are helping but by the good itself residing with that person. And since the Lord is present within all virtue and godliness, their affection for what is good bears witness to their love for the Lord as well. When they are moved at heart by charity such as this, they are regenerate.   — *Secrets of Heaven* §3688[4]

We must acknowledge that no person is his or her evil and that we should not attribute evil to them. Let's live the belief that, although we do evil, we are not our evils. It is not our business to judge if another person has made an evil his or her own or not. Only the Lord can judge that.

So Work on yourself. As we continue in the Work, more and more we will see the good to love in our neighbor, and we will also see the evil from which we can help free our neighbor in any way possible.

What Charity Requires

Earlier in this book, we discussed the importance of elevating our lives into the rational mind. From there, we can be objective about ourselves and see from truth the nature of our lives and our own states. However, if we go up into the rational mind and remain in truth alone that does not have good in it, then we can be used by truth alone, which is very judgmental and condemning:

> A rational mind devoid of life received from heavenly good . . . fights with everyone, and everyone fights with it. Virtue in the rational mind never fights, no matter how much it is assailed, because it is gentle and mild, long-suffering and yielding, for its nature is that of love and mercy. But although it does not fight, it nevertheless conquers all.
>
> — *Secrets of Heaven* §1950[2]

There is a great difference between coming from truth alone (or a selfish love or your own intelligence) and coming from a good affection.

Charity requires that we have real (or positive) love for others and for the good in them. Real, positive love cannot be turned into selfish desires. Real love goes beyond requirements that IT sets (such as money, attractive looks, etc.). Selfish loves always have requirements; true love has none. You can love the good in a person no matter what he or she is.

If we experience positive love, we will have a sense of how strong the Lord's love is for everyone. There are people who would jump in front of a car to push a child out of the way. There are people who would go to prison to save someone else. There is the capability of being willing to give up the self, and even our life, for the sake of someone we love. Concentration camp survivors tell of the incredible compassion and humanness they sometimes saw. Positive, unselfish love is possible, and I am sure you have seen it at some time in your life.

The Lord truly loves the neighbor. It is only the Lord within us that is capable of loving the neighbor. That is why the process of spiritual growth is a re-forming of the whole person. When IT is made quiescent within a person, the Lord can give that person new states that can love the neighbor.

To truly love our neighbor, we have to experience them. For me, external considering is only a beginning step. Whenever I do external considering, putting myself in the neighbor's place or shoes, so to speak, I do not yet come to loving him or her, because I am just barely beginning to realize there are other people on the planet, which I was oblivious to beforehand! We must learn to experience our neighbors not from our selfish I's or selfish loves, but from the part of ourselves where the Lord resides.

In addition to experiencing our neighbors, and having good affections toward them, charity requires that we use justice in dealing with the evil in other people.

Justice never involves revenge. When you watch television or see violent movies, you will notice that these stories often make it seem acceptable to seek revenge. Often they show the good guys reaping revenge on the bad guys as if that is a good thing to do. These stories give permission for the evil to get their just deserts, so to speak.

Actually, there is nothing good whatsoever in an attitude of revenge. Revenge, in fact, is one of the worst sins. Earlier, we saw that Jesus instructed us to love those who hate us; Swedenborg echoes this sentiment:

> People of depth . . . do not want evil to be repaid for evil; instead, they pardon wrongdoers with heavenly charity.
> — *Apocalypse Explained* §556[8]

Sometimes, it is difficult to see how to love a neighbor justly. For example, how can you love an alcoholic without enabling them? How can you really love someone who is leading a disordered or evil life without contributing to the disorder or evil?

The answer is to keep saying "No!" to the manipulative behavior that has the person enslaved and subservient. Look beyond the manipulation and see someone who is stuck; you don't want to add to it or feed that behavior, because if you do you will get that person even more embedded in their destructive behavior! If you feed the negativity that has them unable to break out, you are only encouraging it. If you don't cooperate with their negativity, it may holler and scream and accuse you of being the problem. The negatives holler and scream because you are refusing to help them grow further.

As was said before, it is key that we Work on ourselves first. When someone who has never had a problem with alcohol tries to help an alcoholic, they often find they cannot help the alcoholic. Often the person trying to help judges the alcoholic or condemns the situation. On the other hand, recovering alcoholics with six or seven years of sobriety will generally be very loving to alcoholics, but they will also be very clear about what is necessary for recovery. Recovering alcoholics who have been sober for several years have already been where the alcoholics are. This is an example of how first working on the self eventually results in being able to really help a neighbor with similar problems.

It is difficult when action is demanded, but we do not have that new place in ourselves to come to yet, where the Lord acts through us. That is the reason that noncritical observation of ourselves is the perfect Work for right now. To learn about the nature of various kinds of negativity, we have to free ourselves from them.

Examining and seeing our own evils will provide us with the strength and guidance needed when we interact with someone in disorder. It will be a perfect example of what the Lord can free us from. At this stage, we can ask questions about ourselves, not about the other person, when we are dealing with bad behavior and problems with others. We learn through them about our own imperfections.

On the other hand, charity also demands that we protect ourselves and others from evil when necessary.

In Jerusalem, Jesus cleansed the temple of the money
changers:

> Then Jesus entered the temple and drove out all who were sell-
> ing and buying in the temple, and he overturned the tables of
> the money changers and the seats of those who sold doves.
> — *Matthew* 21:12

Jesus did not cleanse the temple because he was angry with
the money changers. He cleansed the temple in order to
salvage it for the people who were coming to worship, who
were being robbed and prevented from worshipping.

Charity also sometimes requires the punishment of evil—
not revenge, but a just punishment for the sake of preventing
repeated offenses:

> Those governed by evil are likewise the neighbor, but . . . good
> is done to them if they suffer the punishments prescribed by the
> laws, because these punishments serve to correct them, as well
> as to prevent evil from being done to the good by them and the
> bad examples they set.   — *Secrets of Heaven* §5008[3]

When a good judge sentences someone to jail, the judge
does not do it to punish the bad; she does it to help the good
in that person. If the judge could, she would leave the good
part out of jail and send only the bad part to jail. But
unfortunately, the judge has to send the whole body to jail.
She hopes that the good will be shaken loose from the evil
and that the person will start to see that evil has had dominion
over him or her and make a separation. That shaking loose is
the end and purpose of the punishment.

In addition to protecting the worshippers, Jesus punished the
money-changers for their own sakes, because the good part of
them had been taken over by evil. Perhaps at first they had
gone to the temple to sell animals for use in worship; but at
some point, the means became the end. The money became
the end, and the worship became the means. That reversal of

values or loves, or turning things upside down, was now the money-changers' usual condition, and Jesus came to free them from that condition.

If We Truly Believed

We are told that the Lord is in the least of the least. Providence isn't just a big organization with a chairman of the board and several managers, with everything falling apart down in the details. We may sometimes think that things fall apart in the details, because that is how our own lives seem, but it is not true.

Our very lives are the Lord's, and the Lord is present in each life. If he was not living in our little fingers, they would die and fall off. He is here, even in the interactions between people that we think of as less than we desire. He foresaw the lives of each of us from eternity to eternity.

What prevents us from trusting the Lord, who is all love, all wisdom, and is seeing from eternity to eternity? Intellectually, we know about providence, and we are trying to make our belief a living reality. We need to ask ourselves, "How would I behave differently if I truly believed that the Lord's providence is in every detail of my life, my children's lives, and everyone else's life?" We need to live as if we have that belief, and in time we will actually have it, if we get rid of the things that stand in the way.

The Lord is always presenting us with the perfect opportunity to see what we need to work on, as Maurice Nicoll explains:

> Without knowledge of our Being, it is impossible to work on Being. . . . [O]ne sign of a higher level of Being is the capacity to bear the unpleasant manifestations of others. One does not continually get negative with other people.[1]

---

1. Nicoll, *Commentaries*, 1035.

Let's also consider the following quotes, which say that if you understand someone, you agree with that person. If you do not agree with him or her, you do not understand them:

> [Ouspensky wrote:] "*[Y]ou cannot understand and disagree.* In ordinary conversation we say very often: 'I understand him but I do not agree with him.' From the point of view of the system we are studying this is impossible. If you understand a man you agree with him: if you disagree with him you do not understand him. It is difficult to accept this idea and it means that it is difficult to understand it."[2]

> Violence is the antithesis to Understanding. All violence has its roots in not understanding another. . . . [N]egative emotions do not lead to understanding but to violence. The more negative you are the less you understand and the more violent you tend to be. . . . Understanding is a positive thing. . . . [N]egative emotions never speak the truth. They are liars—often very clever liars—but always liars. If you are in a negative state, then everything is distorted and you understand nothing or misunderstand everything. . . .
>
> Now it might be said that when you get violent you come to the limit or end of your Being. Capacity for endurance is a sign of Being.[3]

There is such a thing as negative doubt, and also there is positive doubt. One leads to all disharmony and the other to all understanding. The best attitude assumes this: *Even if I don't understand, I will keep a positive attitude and wait to understand.* We can have a positive attitude like that toward other people.

The Work says the easiest thing in the world is to disagree. It is the lower level mind's immediate response or nature. If

---

2. Nicoll, *Commentaries*, 1036.
3. Nicoll, *Commentaries*, 1039, 1041.

you say, *Yes*, IT says, *No*. If someone says, *Good*, IT says, *Bad*. IT does that automatically and immediately and continually, with no effort and no attention. It is the easiest thing in the world to disagree with people.

If we truly believed in the Lord's providence, then we might see that the person with whom we disagree is also part of God's plan and has a place in providence. By approaching that person through our Work on ourselves, we adopt a positive attitude and turn disagreement into harmony.

Task Choices for Chapter 10

Choice 1

The first task option is to elevate your mind into understanding or agreement with your neighbor, remembering that, if you understand someone, you agree with him or her, and that if you do not agree with that person, you do not understand him or her.

Even the statement of the task is easy for IT to disagree with, so do not relate to people from that part of your mind, because IT disagrees with everything. Use effort and attention to raise yourself into a part of your mind that can think above the natural level.

When you do the task, ask yourself, "How could I understand this in such a way that I would agree with it? In what way or attitude could I bring my understanding into agreement with such-and-such statement or person?" In trying to come to acceptance, you are going to have to leave one level of understanding and come to a new level.

To grow spiritually, it is essential not only to imbue one's spirit with truths, but to use effort and attention to see life from those truths. You can get a lot out of effort and attention, or what the Work calls "long thinking." Also, of course, you need to have good affections for the Lord and the neighbor. We need to learn to love our neighbor as our self.

Choice 2

An alternate task is to be aware of how you relate to your neighbor. Are you relating from IT or from a higher place? Can you see that your neighbor is not the bad habits he or she has? Do you relate to your neighbor while being aware that IT is active in that person, but that IT is not him or her? From what part of your mind do you relate to your neighbor? Of course, at one time you may relate from a better place than at another time, but in general, how do you relate to that person? Or in particular, at a certain time?

CHAPTER 11
Removing Barriers

Love is cancelling all debts.
— *Maurice Nicoll*

*E*manuel Swedenborg wrote that reflection is an important
part of the spiritual growth process:

> The doctrine of faith accomplishes nothing at all with people
> unless the Lord enables them to reflect. That is the very reason
> why people learn what is true and good from the Word of the
> Lord, namely, so that from what they learn, they may reflect
> upon themselves. . . . It is of the utmost importance, therefore,
> to learn truths. Without spiritual knowledge, there can be no
> reflection, thus no reformation. . . .
>
> The doctrine of reflection is an entire doctrine, and with-
> out it no one is able to know what inward life is, not even what
> the life of the body is. In fact, without reflection from a knowl-
> edge of truths, no one is reformed
> — *Spiritual Experiences* §737; §739

Reflection is like seeing yourself from someone else's point of
view, or objectively. This takes effort. In therapy, it might take
a year to get to know someone at any depth. Psychoanalysts say
it often takes five years before a person gets to know him-
or herself.

Usually we don't see ourselves objectively; instead, we look at other people and judge them from our own point of view, which is subjective fantasy. Swedenborg stated that we must "reflect upon ourselves from [the viewpoint of] others, or allow others to reflect upon us, and to say what we are like, . . . [so that] for the first time we are able to know ourselves. Otherwise, we can never learn, but remain in our own illusions, and from them, reflect upon others" (*Spiritual Experiences* §734).

To get an idea of what reflection is, Swedenborg suggested putting your attention on one part of your body and becoming aware of the sensation there (*Spiritual Experiences* §733).You will be aware of a sensation only if you reflect upon that part of the body. For example, consider breathing. Without consciously thinking about breathing, you are unaware that you are doing it. Once you are conscious of it, however, you can feel the breath going into your lungs and your lungs expanding.

Reflection can help us choose between good I's and bad I's in ourselves. Consider the difference between "zeal" and "anger." Zeal, as explained in Swedenborg's writings, is a very different experience from that of anger. Zeal is a passion for a truly good cause, a good state, while anger is a passion for an evil cause. Zeal is more mild, even though it may be persevering. Zeal may appear to be similar to anger, but the difference exists in the internal state. For example, say your young child runs into the street and you run after her and pull her safely back onto the sidewalk. As you tell your child how dangerous her behavior was, you may appear angry even if your internal state is good—you are experiencing a state of zeal that is motivated by the fear of a loss of good (your child's life). This is a very different kind of state from anger, which might motivate you to yell at your child even after he or she understands that what she did was dangerous. Zeal propels us toward caring about another in a good way, while anger separates us from that person, forces us to seek control over him or her through intimidation or shame.

There is a distinction you can make to tell which I's are which. If you have an internal monologue that says anything evil about anyone, it is a bad "I" speaking. As Maurice Nicoll has written, "Once you begin to have negative emotions against another person, whom you say you love, and enjoy [those emotions] secretly, you are making it impossible to have relationship. Love is canceling all debts."[1]

When we are governed by the Lord and new, good states are active in us, we are in a very advanced state. But before that, we may find that we are being governed by our negative I's, having evil thoughts and feelings. We may also find ourselves doing things that we know are wrong—in other words, we may be sinning. We might even try to grow spiritually on our own (and, of course, we would not succeed).

If we can observe an evil within ourselves and separate from it, we can resist the evil by allowing the Lord to resist it for us. If we do not identify with an evil or think that we are the negative or evil state, then *our inclination to that evil is not attributed to us, nor is it considered a sin*:

> If people were to believe as things really are, which is that everything good and true comes from the Lord and everything evil and false from hell, they could not have been found guilty of any offence or had evil ascribed to them. But because they believe that it begins in themselves, they take evil as their own; for their belief causes this to happen. Thus evil clings and cannot be separated from them.   — *Secrets of Heaven* §6324

It would be easy for us to grow spiritually if we attribute neither good nor evil to ourselves. Attributing evil to ourselves is identifying with it and acting from it. We want to have a non-identified relationship to evil thoughts and feelings, even though it is difficult not to be actively involved in what we

---

1. Nicoll, *Commentaries*, 1057.

think and feel. We also want to have good affections and not be identified with them or take credit for having them.

The situation is as though we are a telephone: any thought or feeling can speak through us. Despite this, when a negative thought or feeling speaks through us, we feel it is us, which is not true. To be non-identified during that phone use would be to know immediately that it is not we speaking, to choose not to support it in any way, and to separate from it by thinking and knowing that IT is not us. The importance of this correct reaction to negative input cannot be over-emphasized.

The Two Components of Understanding

The task for chapter 10 concerned understanding and agreeing with the neighbor. The most important part of that task is beyond thought. Without any Work, we really do not understand other people. IT doesn't understand other people. If we live from the realization that we must use effort and attention to understand other people, we will make a major change in our lives.

Understanding, according to the Work, has two components: knowledge and being (or essence).

Having knowledge is simply knowing something that is true. An example is having an awareness that a Work tool like "stop thought" or "external considering" can help us grow spiritually. Being (or essence) is different. A person's level of being can be described by the kinds of states that person experiences. Nicoll gives an example of constantly losing our temper at a certain point. It doesn't matter how much knowledge we have, if we lose our temper, then we have reached the limits of our being.[2]

Understanding links knowledge with being. For example, to raise our level of being, it may first be necessary to acquire new knowledge (such as the tool "external considering"). Then, by Working with that knowledge, we can actually gain a better

2. Nicoll, *Commentaries*, 1434.

understanding of someone else or our situation with them, and experience better states (because we are refraining from identifying with an angry thought, for example).

Ideally, a person has being and knowledge equally, but this is rarely the case. Often our knowledge is beyond our being. For example, often we know how we would like to behave in certain situations, but we don't really live up to our ideals. So having different levels of knowledge and being within the same person can cause problems.

Problems can also result when different people with different levels of knowledge try to understand one another.

Consider this example. Another person and you could have totally different knowledge if one of you grew up in Africa and the other grew up in the United States. One of you might have much knowledge of computers, and the other might have extensive knowledge of medicinal plants. If you were to talk with each other about either of those subjects, in order for you to have an understanding of each other, you would both have to gain all the knowledge the other person has. We are not even talking yet about agreeing or disagreeing with each other. We are talking about just getting the same base of knowledge. To get to a common base of knowledge would take effort and attention.

In a different situation, a person might know everything you know, and in addition, know a lot of things you don't know. Let's say you start on a new job in the computer industry, and there is someone there with seniority of twenty years. After you get attached to the program you just wrote, that person with greater experience might look at your program and say, "No, no, no." Then what has to happen? Well, if you wish to understand, you are going to have to increase your knowledge so that you can talk to that person from a similar knowledge base.

What if the situation is the other way around? What if you happen to know a lot more than another person, and your disagreement with them comes from somewhere within your knowledge, which they lack? What would you have to do in order to understand the other individual or come into agreement? One option would be to communicate only at their level of knowledge.

Here's an example. Suppose you go into your child's room, and she says, "Dad, it's awful dark. I think there is a ghost in here." You could, from your greater knowledge, say, "Don't be stupid! There isn't a ghost in here! Now go to sleep and stop bugging me!" Or, you could go over to her, pretending you don't know anything about anything, and say, "Wow, you really look afraid. What are you afraid of?" She might say, "Over there is a ghost." You could say, "Perhaps you're right! You mean that thing over there that looks like it has its arms out straight? That is frightening!" She might say, "Yeah!" You could ask her, "Want me to go over there and flip on the light and see if it goes away?" She'd say, "Yeah, do it, but be careful!" You could flip on the light and say, "Oh, look at that! It is only your robe. That had me a little nervous! Let's check out the rest of the room while the lights are on, okay?"

In psychotherapy, this kind of process is called "pacing and leading." Milton Erikson, the great therapist and hypnotist, used pacing and leading even on very sick patients. If he had a patient who hadn't said a word in ten years and who just sat in a chair rocking back and forth, Erikson would not say to his patient, "Look, this is ridiculous, and you are wasting your time rocking." Instead, he would sit down and start to rock with that patient until he had the rock just right, until he got his body language in sync, and until his breathing and his eyes matched the patient's. When he had it all just right, when he had come to experience fully his patient's experience, then the patient, even if he or she couldn't talk, would probably feel understood. Erikson would then be in agreement with that person's experience, which is called being in rapport with them, and *then* something further would be possible. From that point, Erikson could lead and expand his patient's knowledge toward his own knowledge level because the patient would follow along.

When knowledge between two people is even, one person can lead or expand a subject. If knowledge is uneven, two people can disagree because one doesn't know something; the two people cannot understand each other, and most likely will disagree.

Suppose someone has knowledge of a particular situation or subject that you don't have, and you have some knowledge he doesn't have. In addition, you both share some knowledge. If you both want to understand each other, you both have to expand your knowledge to include that of the other, or you both have to become passive to all the knowledge you have that the other person lacks. Then you could come into agreement with each other's experience of life, and you could both understand.

I was at a stop light recently and the light changed, but the person in the car in front of me was busy looking down at something, and his car did not move. I felt impatience and anger about that. I started thinking, "You stupid so and so . . ." I knew something he didn't know: that it was time to move! But I tried giving up that knowledge, becoming passive to it, trying to experience his state, how he was trying to make a decision from reading a map as the light changed. Immediately, the feelings attached to my greater knowledge, and my disagreement with him, disappeared.

Since trying to do the task for Chapter 10 and noticing my own automatic disagreements with people on television and my reactions to people in person, I have come to realize that I do not have enough information about or understanding of other people to judge them. When I saw that, my negative emotions towards other people disappeared. Of course, I must make that effort or have that insight again and again, with each new negative reaction.

So we do not understand each other. One reason we disagree with others is that our knowledge is uneven.

Another serious problem is the tremendous amount of negative emotions that are attached to our disagreements. Not understanding other people causes a great deal of upheaval from negative emotions. IT is often active, and IT can't disagree without having negative emotions, because IT wants to rule. And when we operate from IT, of course we can't agree with other people. IT doesn't even like other people!

In addition, people often react to their reactions to each other. If two people are asleep, spiritually, one person will respond automatically to the other, who will in turn respond automatically to the first person's automatic response. Many of our reactions will disappear once we realize that they occur not in response to actual people, but to our own fantasies. We so often project thoughts and feelings, good or bad, onto the neighbor. Sometimes we can even feel that neither of us is relating to the other—we are both relating as if each of us were someone else.

We have to accept and be aware of the fact that we do not really know other people and that our reactions often are not to people themselves. When a misunderstanding occurs, instead of focusing on the misunderstanding, it would be better if we could notice the negative emotions attached to the disagreement and Work on them. To get along with others instead of disagreeing, we can shift our knowledge to help the understanding a bit, but also we need to Work on the negative emotions that block love. We need to do the Work and separate from IT. In other words, we need to raise our level of being by Working.

We saw above that two people with different knowledge can communicate if the person with greater knowledge begins communicating at the other person's level. We can make the same case in regard to being. If someone with greater being wants to understand you, he will not try to relate to you from his greater being, but will come to see what your life is like from your state and begin relating to you from that point. Jesus did that constantly with us during his time on earth. He forgave people so many things. He understood what each life was like at our low level of being.

If we could relate to the neighbor *without* coming from IT (which is almost impossible at our present level of being), we might be able to disagree without any heat or negative emotions involved. If we could always attribute the best motive possible to the neighbor, we would have real love for them.

Giving Up What is Not You

The Work says that IT must be quiescent in order for the Lord to be active in us. The Work also talks about us being "nothing." Plato once wrote, "I neither know nor think that I know."[3]

After you have been Working for a while, you realize that negative I's in you use the phone, and that phone is a vessel called *you*. We have always thought that we each are one person instead of a multiplicity of I's. Still, we take on all the different moods and attitudes that come through us, as if they are us. We defend them and try to make them right or prove them right. It takes observation to see what is really going on. What we take as us is not us at all.

If you observe the voice on your phone, then you will be able to see that a lot of things that you thought were good and true (such as your likes and your dislikes) aren't good or true at all. They are just petty negative I's that have selfish loves and love of the world, anger and impatience, contempt, and many other bad traits.

You will find that things start to change if, instead of thinking your negative I's are you, you stop identifying with the negativity within you. You can stop thinking that IT is you. You can feel that you are "nothing"—you are certainly not the negative I's on your phone—and IT can be quiescent.

---

3. Plato, "An Aplogy," in *Selected Dialogs of Plato: The Benjamin Jowett Translation/Revised, and with an Introduction by Hayden Pelliccia* (New York: The Modern Library, 2000), 288.

There comes a point in the Work where you feel you are giving up everything that is *you*. But the real truth is you have to give up or die to all the things that are *not you*.

The Lord gives you only what can lead to your own and everyone else's spiritual welfare. Letting him lead is to become "nothing." When IT is quiescent, the Lord can act through you; he can do something brand new.

And you will feel something brand new happening. From your new state, you will observe your life from doctrine, from the truth, seeing things the way they really are. You will come to understand yourself in a way you never understood before. You will no longer have the same things bothering you and the same old arguments with other people coming up again and again. The truths you knew but could not formerly live from (because of negative things in the way) become enlivened when the Lord becomes active within you. Then those truths actually become part of your life, instead of just truths in a book or truths in your head.

In this new state, you gain much from a spiritual point of view. You will find the Lord resisting things for you that you were not formerly able to resist. You can experience a vertical change, a true increase in your level of being, instead of the usual horizontal shifts. All the things that formerly were so important—like riches, and reputation, and honor—don't matter so much any more. Somebody steals your money, and now you give the thief your coat also. You are coming from a place totally different from the one you used to come from in regard to life. Your new focus is on being lifted up spiritually.

But if we do not separate from IT, these changes will not happen. As long as we are full of the self, busy justifying IT, defending all the false pictures we have of how we are, the Lord cannot act through us. IT can produce nothing of good.

When we talk about becoming quiescent, we are talking about IT becoming quiescent, not our lives. The Lord will take care of you, and you will probably appear more active in life, if you Work, even though inside IT is becoming quiescent.

In folklore there are many stories about people who are not what they appear to be. A prince appears to be a beast in *Beauty and the Beast*. Snow White appears to be dead after she eats the poisoned apple. The people in these stories often are born to kings and queens but somehow come to have a spell cast over them, or suffer some other misfortune, and they are not what they seem.

The real part of us, the essence or being part of us, is like the prince or the princess we really are. As Maurice Nicoll explains, "The Work says we are born as Essence. As very little children we are in Essence. But Essence, which is the real part of us, is very small, primitive and undeveloped."[4]

What we think is a beast (our being, or essence) is a prince, and what we think is a prince (IT) is really a beast!

There can be a slow change and a discovery, if we Work. The Lord is creating something in us that really is something, and we will be given the experience of it. We cannot have that experience while we are full of our self, but we can have it if we are willing to do the Work.

In a sense, our whole spiritual life is about sleeping, awakening, and being awake. Those are the three spiritual states we go through. Divine revelation and the Work are paths to spiritual awakening.

When we are spiritually asleep, we react from IT, automatically and with no effort and no attention. By studying divine revelation and the Work, we gain new ideas, such as the concept that each of us is not one I but a multiplicity of I's, that we are often identified, and that applying these ideas to our lives causes us to change. This change is called repentance. Rather than seeing from fantasy, we begin to see ourselves objectively.

What is the first thing we become aware of or awake to? We become awake to the fact that we are spiritually asleep! We become conscious that we are, for the most part, unconscious

---

4. Nicoll, *Commentaries*, 1112.

spiritually. We become aware that we are mechanical in our reactions. We are just barely waking up from our spiritual sleep. Upon occasion, we are awake for a few minutes, meaning that we become aware of our mechanical reactions. We really do not yet even know who we are, but we are starting to know who we are *not*. Even our good emotions are suspect. For example, often we like other people because of our self. We like people who like us, who dress like us, who talk like us. If someone with blue hair walked into the room right now, we might not know her, but we probably would not like her. If she went into a certain part of the city, where there were others like her, without even knowing each other, they would probably like each other. That is the nature of IT.

Can we do anything about our mechanical reactions? No, we cannot. Suppose someone sees, for example, that she lies all the time. She decides to give it up. She stops for a few hours, then goes back to lying as usual. And if she tries long enough to give up lying, she will come to realize that she can't do it. She is still asleep spiritually, but she has accomplished one thing: *she is conscious of being unconscious.* That is the germ that starts spiritual growth, and it is the beginning of repentance.

So at this stage, we are not going to be able to change our lives immediately. We are not going to be able to stop doing certain things, and we are not going to be able to love people automatically.

We cannot just make ourselves do those things immediately, and that is all right. There is a difference between a drunk being drunk and a drunk that is in a bar crying because he is aware and ashamed that he is always drinking and is in the bar. There is a change when the drunk starts to have some remorse. That happens to us when we become aware of how much we lie, have contempt, judge people, and other such things. There is a true remorse about that.

When the remorse helps us to separate from the negative I's that speak through our phone, we are heading in the right direction. Gradually, through self-observation, we begin not to identify, to feel the separation from IT and be aware that negative states are not us. Then, sometimes, we are able *not* to express those negative emotions we found impossible to resist previously. A reforming is starting to take place in us. At this stage, we have some freedom about choosing one I over another. We can go with one and refuse the other. It appears as if we are making that choice, but the truth is that the Lord is doing it within us, within the spaces created by our seeing that we are not our thoughts or feelings. IT is not you or I.

The minute we attribute the good or evil to ourselves we feel the new freedom subside again. We cannot sin as long as we become aware and know that it is not we who are acting. We can choose to let the Lord do things for us, and we can also refuse to let him help us. So, in one way, we have a part in the process of becoming free.

Eventually, as we grow spiritually, a change takes place. When spiritually awake, we respond to life from the truths we know. Because IT becomes quiescent, we experience new states in which we can use the truths available to us. We are free! Then we do good from a love of doing good. That is the long-term goal.

Gaining Strength

What kind of I would be interested in interfering with our doing real spiritual work? We have thoughts and feelings, but the Work is to judge them; they are not to judge the Work. If we are trying to do the Work from our own power, it will not prosper.

We need to bring divine revelation to the thought or feeling that we are having and see it from that truth, from what revelation tells us about it. Only revelation, or truth from doctrine, can tell us whether an I is good or bad. So, we want to apply doctrine to our thoughts, feelings, and actions, and see what the truth from doctrine can tell us about them.

Here is an example. Suppose you are watching little children playing a soccer game. One little boy just misses making a goal, and his coach comes out and talks to him in a loud voice. You might have a whole series of thoughts about the coach: that he is being too harsh, that he is a mean person and too focused on winning, etc. But if you are Working, you can observe your thoughts and see that they are automatic reactions and are not from a good "I" talking. Remembering truths from revelation can help you see that you do not actually know what is going on in the coach's heart and mind: "Do not judge, so that you may not be judged" (Matthew 7:1) and "Why do you see the speck in the your neighbor's eye, but do not notice the log in your own eye?" (Matthew 7:3).

When we go to church and listen to doctrine, we are taking in real spiritual food, actual substance. If we don't do anything with that substance, if we just go on living from IT (in the lowest level of our minds), the spiritual food we have taken in will dissipate. If instead we take that new truth and remember it when we encounter a negative I and use that truth to observe and see that our state is bad, then that new truth can feed us, and we will actually gain strength that can, and will, resist the negative state. That is wisdom.

If you observe yourself and do the Work, you will find that you are doing more Work than you were doing before. If you don't use any of it, and you don't make any effort to use the tasks as tools in your life, well, then you lose your memory of them. The tools are only yours if you are Working.

And as you progress in the Work, there will be times when your Working will not seem to show. When someone is hit in the mouth by a stranger and does not do anything to retaliate, that person is doing a lot! He or she isn't doing nothing; he or she is Working! Read the sermon Jesus gave on the Mount, and you will see that it is all about your state of being:

> "Blessed are the poor in spirit, for theirs is the kingdom of heaven."

"Blessed are the meek, for they will inherit the earth."
"Blessed are the pure in heart, for they will see God."
— Matthew 5:3, 5, 8

This sermon is about the new states in us that will inherit the earth, even though right now those states may appear weak.

Negative thoughts can be very clever. Were we fighting them from IT, which only appears strong, victory would be impossible. That is the reason we are trying to make IT quiescent and let the Lord fight the negatives through us. Only the Lord can fight against the negatives in us and win.

Once we start to let go of our negative I's and let the Lord take over, we will start to become aware of our reactions. Since most of us are presently living from selfish loves and a love of the world, we don't have true or real relationships with people; we have reactions. When we look at a person walking into church, we might consider that we have a relationship with that neighbor. We may have some thoughts or feelings about him, some memory of an interaction, perhaps; but we are not really relating to that person. Rather, we are relating to our own reaction to them or to our idea of them. Actually, it is not even your own reaction, it is IT's reaction to the other person! IT feels something for the person, IT thinks something about the person, and so forth. And the other person does the same about us, from his own reaction. So we seldom relate to others from a higher state rather than from IT, which has selfish loves and love of the world.

It is very important to be aware of and awake to the fact that we have *reactions* to each other, instead of real relationships, and it is vital that we try to free the neighbor from our reactions to him or her. If someone walks by, and we have a negative reaction, there is a way to modify our response. Imagine a television screen divided down the middle. Our immediate, mechanical reaction goes on one side, while the other side displays an experience of the person without your original reaction. On one half of the screen is your opinion from what you have heard about that person, or the fact that the person is not of your political persuasion, or dresses more casually than you do, or some other fact that you like or dislike about that person. On this side, you are relating to your self, to your own likes and dislikes, not to the person. Then on the alternate part of the screen is the real person and your realization that you do not know *anything* for sure about him. You will realize, too, that the person also may be relating to you from their own likes and dislikes, opinions, training, fantasies, etc.

Here is a little exercise. I will mention some names and you can notice your reaction. Observe any thoughts or feelings you may have about the person. The first thing you may observe is that you don't have a big reaction. Why? Because you are already more aware than usual due to this discussion. Here are some names: George W. Bush, Mother Theresa, Marilyn Monroe, Charles Manson, Judy Garland, Norton Goldberg.

You might have noticed that your reaction changed as you read each name. But what was your reaction to Norton Goldberg? He's a person none of you know! Why did you react? It was IT reacting in regard to all of them; it was not you. IT was reacting, whether your reaction was negative or positive.

Eventually, we will be able to communicate with the neighbor from a higher level of being, if we Work, because the Lord wishes us to experience mutual love. First, however, we must learn to separate from IT.

☙

The Task for Chapter 11

The task this time is to become aware of IT's response to other people and then to free people from that response.

Do the task in any way you wish. I often take my response and imagine it being above the person's shoulder, so that I know that it is just my response, not the actual person. You might choose to imagine the split television screen described earlier. Another way to free the neighbor from your response is to refuse to believe that your response has anything to do with the person, since it doesn't. Take any public figure whose life you have seen depicted on television. The program may have told of a scandal, but you do not truly know anything about that person since you've never met him or her. Anything you think is something you would not be allowed to say in a court of law because it is hearsay, and you have no direct knowledge. IT, however, is more than happy to believe any negative thing it hears about another human being. IT can respond by feeling superior, and it feeds on that. If we choose, we can free other people by remembering that we do not know anything about them.

First, our job is to observe and to find out where we are in regard to our reactions to people. We don't try to change anything at this point. If you get discouraged when you see negative reactions in yourself, then observe your discouragement. Just try to see things as they are, from truth, instead of being asleep and living in a fantasy. Even if everything you look at in yourself is terrible, at least you will be *seeing* that it is terrible. That is good.

Remember, too, during this part of the task, that your observation should be non-judgmental. If you see a positive response in yourself, don't feel pride about it, which is probably just attributing it to yourself. And if you see a negative emotion, just observe it as if you were a scientist objectively studying a phenomenon.

Recall the analogy of negative I's using you as a telephone. There have been some good I's using the phone, and there's been a whole lot of bad I's using it. Pretend you are recording the voices that are using your phone. Observation is the first step in the Work.

After you become aware of your response to a person, the next part of the task is to free him or her from your response. Remember that IT is relating and that you are not relating to the real person. You can just give up your response, or you can refuse to act from it. Your response will still be hanging around, but you can choose to *not believe it* and *not use it* to interact.

So first become aware that IT is responding, then free the other person from that response. You might even get a glimpse of the real person.

CHAPTER 12
A Real Sense of Self

The Work teaches us that Real I exists, but cannot be approached as long as Imaginary I dominates us.

— *Maurice Nicoll*

*H*ere is an interesting quote from Nicoll:

> After a time it is quite possible to reach that stage in the Work in which you do not believe so much in yourself as a real person.[1]

We are not "real" people yet in the sense that a real person fulfills the Lord's creation by always letting love of the self serve the higher goal of love of the Lord and of other people. A real person has positive emotions and is capable of feeling someone else's joy as his or her own. A real person can even love an enemy. I certainly can't do that yet.

We are not yet real human beings, but we wish to be. Remember the sentence from Ezekiel quoted earlier, in which the Lord says this:

---

1. Nicoll, *Commentaries*, 804.

A new heart I will give you, and a new spirit I will put within you; and I will remove from your body the heart of stone and give you a heart of flesh.   — Ezekiel 36:26

We are still people with hearts of stone. We see someone on television who just lost his house in a fire, and how much do we care? What happened in a football game is often more important to us. We don't care or feel as much as we might.

However, this is not critical or fatal spiritually since in the quote from Ezekiel God is talking to us as potentials. Potentially we are truly human or "real." At the present time, we are just not there yet.

One of the first things we learned is that we have multiple I's, that we are not simply one person all the time. What we had previously thought was the self, the Work calls Imaginary I. Imaginary I is the feeling that we exist and have unity, when actually we do not. For example, it is my own feeling that I am Peter Rhodes and that I am the same person all the time, the same one who gets up in the morning and goes to bed again at night. However, I may be in a very different mood early in the morning than I am in the evening, and I may talk to my wife in different ways at those times. Thinking that I am one I is imaginary because, when any thought or feeling can talk through me, I am not really one; I am more like a telephone. Since many thoughts and feelings talk through me, I have a multiplicity of I's, of likes and dislikes and attitudes.

Among our multiplicity of I's is one we especially want to cultivate and that is an Observing I.

The first thing that Observing I notices is that the kind of person we imagine we are, we are not. We used to think we were reasonably good, that we never lied, that we never talked behind people's backs, and so forth. Then, by means of Observing I, we begin to find out that isn't true. We do lie and gossip.

Observing I also confirms that we are a multiplicity of I's, that our Imaginary I has likes and dislikes and a lot of different

faces or personalities. Imaginary I has one personality at our
place of employment, another personality for play, another for
a camping trip, another for arguing. Perhaps you have noticed
that you can be in a terrible mood at home, yelling and
hollering, and all of a sudden when the door bell rings,
everyone in the house suddenly has a different personality!
Another proof of these different I's is the fact that you say you
love your husband or wife, or your children, and yet, the next
thing you know, you are yelling at them. How can that be? It
is because we think of ourselves as one person. Our
imagination allows this to happen. Whenever we picture
ourselves being something different than we really are, that
is Imaginary I.

The Imaginary I is the one we have such difficulty with, the
one we have been observing and finding attached to many
negative thoughts and feelings. Imaginary I is the I we are
becoming passive to so that we can eventually come to Real I.
We must continue to use our Observing I instead of identifying
with our negative thoughts and emotions (IT). Maurice Nicoll
explains, "The Work teaches us that Real 'I' exists, but cannot
be approached as long as Imaginary 'I' dominates us."[2]

We have talked a lot about becoming "nothing." Students in
my classes have said, "Wow! First you ask me to give up my
likes and dislikes, then you want me to give up my attitudes,
then to separate from negative emotions. Then you say even
my personality has no right to exist, and that my love for my
friends isn't really love, that it's my own reaction to my friends
loving me. And then you say I'm not even allowed to be angry
at my friends because the anger is not me, and you want me to
give up internal suffering. Are you trying to get rid of me?"

Well, that is exactly right. We each need to separate from
IT, the external part of our natures.

To do this, we must give up our sense of self that says that
everything that we do is from ourselves. The Work repeatedly

---

2. Nicoll, *Commentaries*, 1102.

says that "man cannot do." The truth is that the Lord is life and that we are not, although the Lord allows us to feel life as if it is our own, to feel as if we can do things without the Lord's influence. This feeling that we can do things by ourselves and that life is our own Swedenborg called our "proprium."

We are asked to acknowledge that the Lord is our life, even though we feel that we live from ourselves. In other words, we are asked to acknowledge that the Lord alone is life, even though we have our propriums and are allowed to live "as if" from ourselves.

Usually, we do not live with this awareness that only the Lord is life. When we are living from selfish states (that is, when IT is active), we do not acknowledge the Lord's presence in our lives and the Lord's presence in whatever we do that is good.

To grow spiritually, we must separate from our selfish states or selfish I's (IT) and acknowledge the Lord's presence in our lives. If we do this, we will be given a "heavenly proprium" rather than our usual one; we will have a "heavenly" sense of self that maintains a correct view of our relationship to the Lord no matter what we are doing in our daily lives.

Knowing these things can be tremendously freeing. I have spent a lot of time telling you that we are not IT (our proprium). If we were IT (our proprium), we would be doomed spiritually.

A Growing Sense of Real "I"

Although we have Imaginary I, there is also a Real I that is a part of us. We are trying to separate from IT (our self-centered proprium) or make it subservient, while we encourage new states or Real I to grow. Real I already exists, but mostly we do not live in a state of Real I. If, however, we use our Observing I instead of identifying with our negative emotions, then we get some sense of Real I.

Now at first there isn't a lot of feeling to Real I because Real I is so small, just a little Observing part, but some good feelings and insights come from observing how things really are. This new state is not like real love or mutual love yet, but it is a love of truth and an eagerness to see the truth and to use it lovingly in our lives.

We have to become dead to IT's proprial desires while truly good, new states are being formed. It is easy to say that we have to die to something, but to actually die to it is very hard. We may have an idea that we can give up the old self and then we will be glad to be the new self, but that isn't the way it works. As we learned in Chapter 6, we don't travel easily from Egypt to the Promised Land in one fell swoop. The trip takes forty years! In fact, in the Exodus story almost every Israelite who left Egypt died before the group got to the Promised Land!

The Bible often uses the image of a grain of wheat dying, falling to the ground, getting trampled into the mud, and then lying passively as winter arrives. If that series of events does not happen, the grain will not transform. There is that period called winter where it looks like the grain is dead and nothing is happening. It is cold, still, apparently lifeless. Then, of course, spring comes, and the grain isn't dead at all, and something can be born.

It is the same way with us. Our old selves are dying. We feel as though we are giving up everything that we are. But as Nicoll explains, it is at this point that we begin to revive: "A man must come eventually to the point in which he realizes clearly that he is nothing. Then he can become something. Then the Work takes the place of what he imagined."[3]

Even if self-observation reveals a lot of negatives, still, it is very good that we are observing IT (the proprium), starting to move away from IT, and beginning to realize that IT is not us.

---

3. Nicoll, *Commentaries*, 936.

The Lord told Moses, "I AM WHO I AM" (Exodus 3:14).

In chapter 9, we saw how we can self-remember by raising our consciousness of "I am." It is the Lord's presence in us, the "I am," that we refer to as Real I. The Lord resides in Real I. Real I is not the Lord, but the Lord is within Real I because he is within every effort we make to live better lives.

As we progress spiritually, we will come to know that the Lord is in us. We will feel our old propriums die as we separate from our negative thoughts and feelings, and the Lord will give us new, heavenly propriums that will grow as we continue our efforts in the Work. We are moving toward that state, but for now we are still where we are.

What we are trying to do is expand the place within ourselves where the Lord can live. And what we are grasping onto and holding so tightly to—namely, our old self—is the very thing that is preventing that from happening. When we feel all the negatives around us and try to separate from them, it feels as if we are being annihilated. However, the good news is that a separation is taking place. We have to become "nothing." When we remember ourselves by saying, "I am," that "I am" is a vessel in which the Lord can live in us and also be active through us. The Lord has given us that potential. So to self-remember and say "I am," is saying, "I am a vessel that the Lord can be active in, and IT is nothing."

The Lord resides in Real I. He resides within the internal person, within the heavenly proprium:

> What severs the external self from the internal [is] chiefly self-love. And the chief thing that unites the external self to the internal is love shared with others, which is in no way attainable until self-love departs, for these types of love are complete opposites. The internal self is nothing else than mutual love. The human spirit itself, or soul, is the interior self which lives after death. . . . The things that belong to the internal self are the Lord's, so that one may say that the internal self is the Lord.

> ... The Lord grants a heavenly proprium to angels or people, so
> long as their life has mutual love in it.
>
> — *Secrets of Heaven* §1594[5]

As we let the Lord destroy our prison, we still may hang
onto the bars and scream while being freed. Sometime in the
future, we may have a different feeling about it. However, if we
hold onto IT (our proprium), we are going to find out that IT
can never be gratified. We can never really have what IT
wants, never have the full pleasure that it claims to offer us;
and if we keep hanging on to it, our spiritual lives are in
jeopardy. Give up your present proprium totally because the
pleasure of anger is not really pleasurable, contempt over others
and feeling superior are not really pleasurable, winning against
somebody weaker is not really pleasurable. There is nothing
genuinely good that we are being asked to give up, nothing at
all. The pleasure of the proprium is just an appearance of good.
Some of it appears good—like the love of people based on
their love for you—but it is just selfish love. So we are giving
up that feeling of false pleasure. There is a tale about a maiden
who was in the woods and the prince arrived, wanting to make
her his wife. She grabbed onto her little hut and didn't want to
go. Then later, when she was crowned a princess, she looked
back and wondered why she had fought so hard against leaving
her hut.

Feeling "As If" When in Real "I"

When we become Real I and are in mutual love toward the
neighbor, that is the Lord acting through us, but we get to feel
as if we are acting. So when we say "I am," we are saying that
the *Lord is*, and he gives us the benefit of feeling *as if I am* the
good new state (or heavenly proprium).

So, I am (or the Lord is), and IT is nothing. We can't have
the feeling of *I am* while IT (the proprium) dominates. We
have to come to see IT for what it is and start to separate from

it and have the awareness that we can only have a feeling of *I am* separated from that which we abhor, which is our old proprium.

Shortly before he was arrested, Jesus said to his disciples:

> "If you love me, you will keep my commandments. And I will ask the Father, and he will give you another Advocate to be with you forever. This is the Spirit of truth, whom the world cannot receive, because it neither sees him nor knows him. You know him, because he abides with you, and he will be in you.

> "I will not leave you orphaned; I am coming to you. In a little while the world will no longer see me, but you will see me; because I live, you also will live."   —John 14:15–19

The quote opens by describing a move from where the Lord is not, to where He is. Jesus begins by saying, "You will keep my commandments," which means to try to move away from IT (the old proprium) and separate from it, so that it does not dominate us.

Jesus said that the world didn't know him but that he would send someone to us. He said that the world doesn't know him "but you know him." "The world" that doesn't know him is IT, the old proprium. Our external, proprial selves do not know the Lord because they are incapable of knowing the Lord and incapable of loving the neighbor. IT is incapable of living the truth. "But *you* know him"—you, the *I am*, the internal person, the new person or new good states, the heavenly proprium, or Real I—that part knows him. The Lord has created us so that he can reside in us and become one with us.

We are a bunch of ITs or propriums trying to do the Work. But remember, the Lord is actually doing all the work. We are not really doing any of it, even though our propriums constantly try to make us think we are doing the Work. It appears that we have life, that ideas come to us and we share them, but that is all an appearance. There is only the Lord;

what appears to be our life is actually the Lord's life acting through us.

There is only God, and that is the point. Everything else is only an appearance of life because of God's being within us. We have the appearance of Working, but if any Work gets done, he is doing it. He is knocking on the door constantly, and we spend most of our time trying to keep the door closed in case he might get in. We are just a vessel, and he is reforming us. To the degree that we realize we are actually doing nothing, to that degree he can do even more of the Work through us. He allows us to appear to Work, and we must do what we can, knowing that we do nothing of ourselves.

Acknowledging that it is totally the Lord who lives and acts is vital, but the appearance is otherwise because he wants us to have the feeling of life as long as we acknowledge it is his. Anytime we look from one level to a higher level, the truth appears as a paradox; to a great degree, that is the reason we cannot totally understand. That is also the reason that positive faith is so important—to believe and to accept when we do not totally understand. How can we be doing nothing when we are told that we must do what we can? If we were in a higher state of wisdom, we would understand completely. For now it is a paradox.

Even words appear as a paradox because of our inner states. I sometimes look back and re-read a certain passage from the Work concerning non-identification, a passage that means a lot to me, and I'll think, "That passage meant a lot to me years ago and it means a lot now, but it doesn't mean the same thing. It is still as meaningful, but now it means something entirely different."

Do you have a favorite poem? Each time you read it you may get something more or different from it, even though you thought you understood it the first time, and maybe you did. Then next time, next year, you may think it is the first time you ever really understood that poem.

Let me tell you a story that embodies some of the things we have discussed in this chapter.

Once there was a small acorn that fell out of a big oak tree. The little acorn landed on the ground, right next to another larger acorn. The little acorn looked around and asked, "Now that we are here, what are we meant to do?"

The other acorn, glancing up at the big oak tree, said, "We are meant to become one of those."

The little acorn said, "You gotta be kidding! What are you talking about? That tree is one hundred feet high, and its branches are forty to sixty feet wide! The leaves are ten times bigger than I am! I don't have a prayer of growing into that."

"All I know," said the other acorn, "is that's the deal."

So the little acorn started pushing and squeezing around inside his shell, doing exercises. He thought to himself, "I'm never going to make it," but he kept trying as hard as he could. He thought something certainly should be happening during the summer because he was working so hard trying to grow. He got very discouraged, however, as fall came and the weather got colder and colder.

Then one day a big furry animal came and picked him up, ran into the field, dug a hole, shoved him into it and pawed dirt back over him. The acorn thought, "Hold on! This is very bad. Not only am I failing at what I'm supposed to do, but now I don't have any sunlight, and I don't even know if I am upside right or upside down. It's hopeless!" He felt the frost form around him. He felt himself freezing to death. He said to himself, "It's no use. I can't do it. It's hopeless. I'm just going to give up and die."

Of course, as spring came, he started to have some feeling. As the weather got warmer, the amazed acorn thought, "This isn't so bad. I'm alive! I'm no oak tree, but I'm still here!" So, he popped up with hope, but then, as he looked up at the big oak tree, he once again thought, "I can't do it. I don't even know how I made it through the winter. I didn't do anything, but here I am! Thank the Lord! But there is no way I'm going to become a great oak tree. In fact, I'm going to give it up completely. I'm going to stay right here in this field, and I'm going to drink rain water and sunbathe all summer long." And that is what he did.

Can you guess the ending?

What the acorn did is like what we are each asked to do. If God created the oak tree and the acorn and if he can actually change an acorn into an oak tree, well, then he can do wonders even with us. The acorn probably could not have done anything else. Certainly he could not have changed into a maple tree. If the Lord created us and got us this far, and if his whole purpose is to make a better spiritual being out of us, do you think he is going to give up now? How could anyone who lives the way you and I do possibly make it to heaven? The answer is: *we contribute nothing to the process.*

Remember the acorn. He thought he was a failure. He was not a failure. He felt powerless. He was right. Every jot and tittle, every hair of our heads, every experience of our lives is orchestrated to bring about the changes that the Lord wants to have happen. There are no mistakes, in that sense, *if we are awake.* If we are asleep spiritually and determined to stay asleep, then he cannot help us. However, if we wake up, every experience we have will lead in the direction the Lord wants to take us.

The Task for Chapter 12

The task is simply to self-remember with the feeling or the words, *I am,* followed by, *and* IT (whatever negative state you are experiencing in your proprium: anger, fear, jealousy, irritation, etc.) *is nothing.*

Suppose you come into a state of impatience. You might be in a car or waiting for a train, waiting for your spouse. Then you self-remember, *I am* (the Lord is present, I am, and the

Lord is within me), *and this impatience is nothing.* Another example might be that you drive by a nice house and feel covetous. Then you remember and say to yourself, *I am and this feeling of coveting is nothing.* Or you get angry, then stop and say, *I am and that anger is nothing.* You are anxious about a job-related situation. *I am and that job concern is nothing.*

Remember the *I am* means that the Lord is with you, that he is within you, and the negative concern or negative state is nothing, although it appears to be something. You can be free from all those negative states that appear to be something but are nothing.

Remember too, if you are doing the task with a lot of heaviness and judgment, you are doing it incorrectly. It should be a light thing in the sense that it frees you and need not depress you. Heaviness and feelings of self-pity or disgust are things to leave behind. Elevation feels light. If something feels heavy you can be fairly sure it is an IT (or proprial) state. If you have a sudden insight, it is never heavy but is light and rising up.

CHAPTER 13
Shock Waves of Truth

Every valley shall be lifted up,
  and every mountain and hill be made low;
the uneven ground shall become level,
  and the rough places a plain.
  — *Isaiah 40:4*

Seeds have been found in the pyramids that are thousands and thousands of years old and yet are still capable of germinating and growing. It can be difficult to predict exactly when a seed is going to grow.

The part of us where real spiritual growth takes place is like fertile ground of which we are not usually aware. In this part, seeds gathered long ago can germinate.

It seems sudden when someone hears some new advice and declares, "That's a good idea. I'm going to do it!" Conversely, when someone decides not to do something, it may seem like a sudden decision. But the seeds for those decisions were planted long before.

Sometimes the way characters behave in stories can serve as seeds for our own understanding. We all easily identify with someone in a story. Even while reading the Bible we may identify with the pharisee or the hypocrite and feel guilty. Or you may identify with the hero. When I hear, "You are Peter, and on this rock I will build my church" (Matthew 16:18), my false pride thinks, "Yes, that's me," and it feels good.

However, our Real I can find meaning in stories without becoming identified in a false or undesirable way. Real I can interpret the actions of characters in some stories, especially those in the Bible, as being like different parts of ourselves. Our essence knows that, our Real I knows that, and it doesn't feel either elated or guilty, no matter how the characters in the story behave. Our Real I simply takes certain seeds of understanding, objectively, from stories or elsewhere, and holds them for later use.

In my job as a probation officer, I often have clients whom I recommend go to Alcoholics Anonymous, Narcotics Anonymous, Gamblers Anonymous, or some other appropriate group. There are different ways that a client can react to the recommendation, but usually a client reacts in one of two ways.

One type of client says, "Do I *have* to go to that AA meeting?"

I respond, "Yes, you do. If you don't go to AA, you go to jail."

My client says, "Why?! It doesn't do me any good. Those meetings are a waste of time. I've been there. Those guys are stupid. They just sit around telling their old stories, and they are addicted to coffee and cigarettes now; in fact, they are addicted to the meetings! You can make me go, but you can't make me like it. I don't need meetings."

Sometimes when I see such clients at a later time, I ask if they made the meeting that week. They say things like, "No. I couldn't go to a meeting after working all day. I put in ten hours that day. I can't go to a meeting after working like that." Sometimes they say, "No! It was icy and snowy out!" Or they might say, "It was my birthday! I don't go to meetings on my birthday!"

The second type of client, when asked if he or she went to the meeting, says, "Of course. I made three meetings this week. I should have made the fourth, and I wanted to, but I didn't."

When asked how the meetings are, they say, "Those people are great. If it weren't for them, I wouldn't have my sobriety. I am actually staying sober!" I might say, "Boy, last week was snowy and icy, and aren't you working long hours at your job this week?" My client would probably answer, "Yeah, well, none of those things ever kept me from going to a bar!"

Invariably, the first type of client gets arrested a few months later for drinking or being on a controlled substance or driving under the influence of alcohol. Even then, my client still doesn't see the need for any meetings.

In this Work, *there is no one to contend with other than yourself.*

You may go to a show and not like it, but usually it is not because the actors are no good. It is not because the director is no good. If you hear a sermon and it seems no good, it may not be because the sermon is no good. Maybe it would be educational for you to take a sermon, get it in print, read it slowly to find the parts that you missed the first time, and then underline the parts that you think have a good point. Ask yourself, "What experience was the minister trying to communicate? How would I use that in my life?"

Some people say, "Yes, but there are good shows and bad shows, and good sermons and bad sermons. It's not just what we bring to it or put into things, that counts."

Perhaps. However, our attitude, our effort and attention, is a major factor.

Good Loves Search for Truth

The quote below is from Swedenborg's *Spiritual Experiences* §5643. The quote discusses how someone grows spiritually when a good love in that person goes looking for a truth. Upon finding the truth, the good love joins with it, and the person then notices that truth in the things that happen in the world around him. For example, someone's good love for little children might join with the truth that little children benefit from being loved. Then the person will see the proof of that truth in the children they know—a neighbor's child blossoming in school as a result of a caring teacher, perhaps, or a niece or nephew growing more confident at sports as a parent encourages them in a loving way.

> We are reborn by means of the truth that faith teaches. . . . The truth that faith teaches is received in our memory, and the good that love embraces is received in our will. By means of the intellect . . . the will looks into the memory and sees that this truth harmonizes with the things it considers good. . . . Then it examines that truth, loves it, and believes it. When this happens, it also speaks and acts on that truth. This unites good with truth in our earthly memory and at the same time in our spiritual memory, and they join together.

This passage goes on to say that, if a good person hears that selfish loves are evil and the good in that person loves that truth, then the good in that person will look for that selfish love in his or her own life in order to expose it. The good love doesn't just look around in general; it looks at specifics and starts to hunt for the selfish love in very small variations of the person's thoughts, feelings, and actions.

> It is similar with self-love. If the truth of faith has taught us that this love belongs to hell and therefore *is* hell, the goodness inside us uses its inner eye to draw itself a picture of self-love as hell—a picture that horrifies it. So as soon as we run into something selfish again, and we sense that it is indeed selfish, the goodness in our will uses its eye to re-examine its picture of hell. The Lord then holds us back from anything selfish, and the more He holds us back, and the purer our goodness is, the more we start to learn. The desire to learn, you see, grows along with the good that love embraces, and it also increases as our goodness increases. In the end we become sensitive to the different

categories and types of self-love and notice them inside ourselves. As a result we become wiser and wiser.

— *Spiritual Experiences* §5644

The more observation you do, the more differentiation you
will get between your states. You will see different forms of
anger, or greed, or whatever you are observing.

Spiritual Experiences also states that everything in nature is a
picture of spiritual change. For example, water can function
like truth; just as water can wear down stone, we can use truth
to wear down IT. IT (our present proprium) is often as hard as
stone.

Pretend that someone has just given you the job of taking
down a three-foot stone wall. The person told you, "There is
no rush about it. Take a few years if you need to, but remove
that wall as best you can."

Well, you might think about how the beating of the ocean
wears stone away, and then rush in the house, get a bucket
of water and throw it on the wall. But then you remember
that the flow of water has to be constant. You might then
repeatedly get buckets full of water and throw them at the
wall for hours at a time.

In the Work, people speak of "the way of the Sly Man." If
Sly Man had the plan or desire to use water to take down a
stone wall, you might think he would divert a stream or
something like that, but no. He would first of all use a sledge
hammer to break the top of the wall in a few places so that
those broken places would hold water like a cup. Sly Man
would then thoroughly wet the top of the wall and just leave
the water to do its work.

What would happen next? First, the water would seep down
into the cracks in the wall. When winter comes, the water in
the cracks will turn to ice, which will expand and break the
wall apart. And in the summer when the wind blows, some
sand and dirt will get carried into those cracks, and maybe
some birds come by who like to sit there eating fruit, and they

might drop some seeds onto the dirt that has fallen into the cracks. The following spring, those seeds will pop up and leaf out, and their roots will start growing down into the crevices, going deep. (Maybe you have seen plants that push up through stones and even break open large rocks.) When rain comes, the plants grow deeper and taller, and when the cold comes again the rock will crumble further, due to the freezing and thawing of the water now deep in the cracks.

After three or four years, Sly Man could go over to that wall and see a great change. He could take the rocks away and build a nice patio or something. He would not need a sledge hammer as he did at the beginning; he would not need anything. He would find that the work of dismantling the wall had already taken place.

How does this story illustrate the role of truth in the process of spiritual growth? The stone wall is like a major spiritual misunderstanding or falsity in your life. If you are struggling against IT (your proprium), you might try applying truth a few times (like those few buckets full of water on the stone wall) and find that not much happens. On the other hand, when we have truth that we hold, if we can hold it during states of cold, for example, guess what is going to happen? That truth is going to expand, and it will make a space where there had not been any space before.

So "the way of the Sly Man" is to make oneself open to truth, then to hold that truth over the seasons (not just during the summer when the living is easy, but through all the seasons), and allow seeds to form and germinate. Holding a spiritual truth over all the seasons, through the bad and good times, during all the ups and downs of life, is what having true faith is all about.

The Lord's whole creation is a picture of spiritual change that is already taking place, right now. The one thing we need to do, however, is to open ourselves to the truth and hold it through whatever states the Lord leads us through. Then we can see how powerfully the truth will act. Anyone who has closely observed a stone wall over time knows what can actually happen.

What do you suppose is the meaning of the sledge hammer in this metaphor of spiritual growth? If you have used a sledge hammer, you know that it creates shock waves. The sledge hammer stands for a shock to your system.

When a spiritual truth is no longer just something you hear in church or read in a book, or just a thought that occurs to you when you are talking intellectually to somebody, but instead that spiritual truth becomes something you actually apply to your life, you are thereby creating a shock. It is often a shock, for example, when truth suddenly comes to your awareness at the very moment that you start to say something mean or untrue about someone else. Truth is a shock if applied right at the moment that you are having a strong ugly feeling or mean thought about someone you love.

If you suddenly see the truth while you are having a negative emotional state, that is indeed a shock to your system, like a sledge hammer hitting a wall.

Changing Our Present State for a Heavenly State

Maurice Nicoll wrote that "one cannot change oneself unless the mind changes. As long as you have the same *mental attitudes*, prejudices, opinions, and so on, you cannot begin to change. . . ."[1]

The inclination to try to change at once is from the proprium. The truth is that you can't change right away, and by observing that fact, you *are* doing something. In time, change will take place as a result of your observation, although self-observation is a life-long process. The Work is about change of state. There is no place to go. Just allow your state to change.

---

1. Nicoll, *Commentaries*, 1124.

Remember the definition of heaven given in Chapter 3? That definition said that when you are happy and at peace, having good communication and feeling close to someone, it's like heaven. It feels like the goodness of the kingdom of the Lord is within you.

Many people think we can go to heaven only after we have died. Actually, we do not find heaven by *going* anywhere. "Going to" heaven is only an appearance. You cannot get to heaven by going anywhere! Heaven *comes to us* whenever we clear out a space for it by separating from our negative thoughts and feelings. Heavenly states then enter and become a part of us.

We can only get to heaven by changing our state. This Work is about going to heaven by changing your state to a new heavenly state, by not living from your selfish proprium.

To change, we need to pay attention to details within our self. We need to watch for more and more differentiations within each general negative state, whether that state is called anger, jealousy, lying, lust, or whatever.

One thing we can do to find out the particulars is to observe our tone of voice, not only our general tone of voice but our tone of voice in particular situations. Notice the slight inflection at the end of your sentences. You may try to shoot off little effects onto somebody else. If you want to make someone feel a little guilty, for example, you will find a sign of that at the end of what you say to him or her.

What attitude is that kind of voice coming from? Name it. That is a very good way of defining it. Then ask yourself and observe what impact that state wants to have on the other person, the one you are communicating with. Does your proprium (IT) want to make that person feel jealous, afraid, embarrassed, or some other demeaning emotion?

Once, just before being interviewed for a job, I read the following quote by Nicoll about "willing" or "wanting to do" what you must do instead of fighting it:

Now, if I *will* to do what I have to do, I will not make inner accounts against others. But if I do what I have to do and all the time think that someone else should do it and that it is unfair that I should have to do it, then I am making internal accounts. ... And this will give rise to endless *inner talking.* ...

Notice your inner talking. Notice what obsesses your thoughts. Taste it and see whether it is negative. Try to struggle with it. ... Try to wake up and do what you have to do *from yourself, willingly.*[2]

I was in a waiting room at the time, scared to death. I was scheduled to go before a board of judges in a matter of minutes. When I read the passage by Nicoll, I told myself, "Okay, I will to have the interview. I really want to talk to those judges." Thinking this way helped, just like that! I felt much calmer.

My experience before the job interview illustrates what the Lord meant when he said, "Do not resist an evildoer" (Matthew 5:39). Any evil (even excessive fear) must be exposed before it can be gotten rid of. We can only truly resist an evil by first looking at it honestly and accepting our state for what it is, and then asking the Lord to resist it for us. If we try to "resist" an evil by not looking at it, by not looking at what the truth of our state really is, then that evil will stay with us (perhaps hidden from our consciousness).

When I read the quote from Nicoll before my job interview, because I was conscious of my anxious state and accepted it for what it was and because I decided I wanted to talk to the judges, I was able to will to do what I had to do.

If we will to do what we must do instead of fighting it, we may even experience a physical difference. With observation, we may notice that, when we are doing something we don't want to do, our breathing is labored. But when we want to do something, our breath comes easily and freely.

Let me give you a quick exercise as an example: Relax and

---

2. Nicoll, *Commentaries*, 1117–1118.

recall a recent time when you did something that you didn't want to do or that you thought somebody else should do. Run that by quickly and remember what that experience was like.

Now use your imagination and run that experience by again, pretending that, rather than having to do it, you really want to do that job. Pretend that you volunteered and that you are happy that no one else gets to do the work instead of you. It is your chance. Notice what you have to give up to want to do work, instead of maintaining your original attitude. This time you are asking to do it, volunteering, thrilled to get to do it.

Now, tell me that this exercise didn't make a difference for you! I am sure it did.

What some of you had to give up was laziness or fear—the laziness of not wanting to do anything, the fear of not doing it right. Or perhaps you had to give up the image of yourself being above having to do such a job. Sometimes you even have to give up the feeling that it is your duty in order to enjoy doing something. You may have to give up resentment in order to want to do it.

Whatever you must give up, giving it up certainly is an improvement, isn't it?

The Work often focuses on the necessity of using effort and attention because, whenever you do not, you will immediately react from and think from IT (your present proprium). That is the human condition.

Emanuel Swedenborg in *Secrets of Heaven* §6210 wrote that there are forces continually dragging our attention downwards, down to merely worldly things. In order to counter those forces, we need to stretch our thoughts and minds toward heaven. Swedenborg also wrote in *Secrets of Heaven* §6201 that, in order for a person to be uplifted, that person must think about eternal spiritual life. If we decide to think about heaven or spiritual life, our state will be uplifted because of our choice or decision.

As we become more aware of our thoughts and feelings, more conscious of our propriums with their negative thoughts and feelings, we can better shun evil and suffering with every breath. We can resist anxiety, the concern for self, and all the other worldly and very present things standing between us and our true aim of spiritual growth.

Who Would Want What You're Giving Up?

The Work says that through self-observation we will come to know our own particular form of suffering. Everybody has his or her peculiar form of it, and the only thing a person can really sacrifice is this suffering.

It may take years and years before you discover your special form of suffering; and when you discover it, you'll have the Work of seeing it, of not identifying with it, of separating from it, and finally sacrificing it. In order to do anything willingly, you have to sacrifice a particular slice of your suffering.

We may have feelings of being owed. If I do this and don't do that, somebody owes me. I don't know whom, but somebody owes me because doing this thing isn't my responsibility, not my job. I worked hard all day, why do I have to feed the dog? Being owed is a feeling of being put upon, of not being estimated at your proper value. We have to give up that kind of attitude.

If at a time of feeling this kind of self-pity (or being owed something), you start to understand that this attitude has to be sacrificed and you actually try to sacrifice it, you will find that doing so is not easy. You might think that someone would give up a feeling of suffering freely since the feelings are negative. But no! We all hold on to our suffering tighter than anything. Nonetheless, these negative feelings are what we must give up. How are we going to do that? It seems impossible.

The truth is that IT can't give up anything negative. That selfish, suffering, put-upon state in you is the very life and delight of IT (your present proprium). And when IT is active, it will feel like your very life! When you are in that state, you feel as if there is no way you could give it up, that you would have to die in order to give up that particular negative thought or feeling. In fact, the only way for your present proprium to give up a negative is to die. (And many people commit suicide rather than give up a negative suffering attitude.)

This is the reason that non-identification is so important. This is why we say, as in the task to Chapter 12, *I am and IT is nothing.*

When saying that phrase, we don't identify as much as usual. When we get a separation of feeling, we can see that IT is nothing, but until then IT is everything! When we see the delight in a negative feeling for what it is, we don't have to give up anything but thinking that the feeling is us! Self-pity does have its delight, and it will share it with us if we are willing to be identified. Until we let our suffering go, we cannot do things willingly, joyfully, from the light and the life of mutual love, from all the things the Lord wishes to give to us. Being identified is the price we pay for wanting to keep negative suffering, the delight of self-pity, the feeling of being put upon.

Once we know that separation is possible, because we have a rational mind we can begin to think rightly, and even say, "IT is angry" or "IT has self-pity." But IT still feels like us. Genuine feelings of separation may come at first only in flashes in regard to states or thoughts we are less attached to, things that are not real big temptations for us. Perhaps just in regard to some small, mean thought about someone, we might be able to come to a separation. Then using that experience as a metaphor, later on in regard to a bigger thing that we are really attached to or identified with, we may be able to separate further. The goal is separation from the negative, to see that negative thoughts and feelings are active in us and to *know* that they are not us. To come to *feeling* they are not us is true separation.

Once we are able not to identify with a particular negative thought or feeling, we will see that the thought or feeling we have given up is, in one sense, nothing, because who else would want what we've given up? Laziness, self-image, duty, labored breathing, selfish loves—we just had a taste of those things in our little exercise. We weren't sacrificing anything when we imagined giving them up, because the things we had to give up were not really ours to begin with. Rather than resisting evil, we can examine it instead.

Sometimes it is useless to argue with negative thoughts or to engage them in any way. It is best to observe negative thoughts or feelings objectively, notice that they have nothing useful to offer us, and then surrender them to God by asking him to take them. God will, at some point, separate the negative thoughts and feelings from us.

Here's an example from my own life. A temptation I have is waking up in the morning and thinking of all the difficult things that are ahead of me that day. I used to spend a lot of time on those kinds of thoughts, trying to figure out how I would deal with the meeting coming up, how I would order the day. I would try by this means to get rid of the experience I call anxiety. However, I found that these efforts only increased my anxiety! After I devised my plan for dealing with the difficult things, I would worry about whether I would remember my plan, whether it really was a good plan, and so on.

When I experimented with just observing and surrendering anxious thoughts, I found that anxiety disappeared. I had tried to contend with anxiety for a long time, but I found out that contending with anxiety doesn't work, because as long as I'm in communication with it, it is too close to me. As long as anxiety is near, I experience it. As long as anxiety can talk to me, it has me within its influence. If I stop talking to it or arguing, anxiety starts to disappear; but then if I think about it or mention it again, the anxious feeling comes right back.

However, when I experimented with observing and surrendering my anxiety, bringing truth to my thoughts and feelings, I saw that they always centered on the concerns of my selfish proprium. I also saw that I could not change myself— that I was powerless over negative thoughts and feelings. Truth shows me that I need to let go of or surrender the selfish concerns to God; then I can not only be freed from them, I can instead be open to thoughts about God and concern for others.

We can gain a state of peace by becoming aware that, although evil will flow into us and we will experience it, *the evil is not us*. Evil is nothing but the absence of good. We can also come into a state of peace by realizing that all the good that comes into us is not us but is from the Lord (even though we are allowed to experience it as if it is our own).

Heavenly peace comes with that double acknowledgment of neither good nor evil being us.

The Task for Chapter 13

The task concerns breaking habits.

Usually, we are so mechanical that we repeat the same experiences over and over again. We have habits of feeling, and we always get indignant the same way or sad the same way or hurt in the same way. Those reactions are just habits.

We have habits of thinking, too. We think the same opinions about politics, or finances, or government. That thinking is just a habit of the mind.

As an allegory or metaphor for breaking our mental and emotional habits and attitudes, we are going to practice breaking physical habits. What physical habits? Every one you can possibly think of. If you usually get up and brush your hair before you bathe, then bathe before you brush your hair. If you brush your teeth with your right hand, brush with your left hand. Start being creative. If you always walk to work, ride. If you always ride, walk.

For the first day, break two or three habits; the next day break five or six. Be willing to have your life be different. You can even try to break some big habits, if you want.

I used to eat lunch at a hot dog stand. When I did this task to try it out, I found myself at noontime in a candlelit restaurant. The week I did this task was a great week. When you do this task, it will give you a little practice in changing.

CHAPTER 14
Impressions Given and Received

Those who have charity hardly notice evil in another person,
but instead notice everything good and true in the person.
— *Emanuel Swedenborg*

Do we trust in divine providence? Recently a friend told
me of a drive to the airport. As he was driving along, he
noticed that his car was running out of gas, and there was no
exit ramp in sight. Besides, he would miss his plane if he had
to detour in order to stop for gas. My friend said that, if we
really trusted in providence we could relax even under those
circumstances; but I noticed that I was anxious even as he was
telling me the story.

So, we might wonder, is it really possible to be relaxed in
such a situation? Of course, it is; but it may take time to reach
that level of trust. It is a good long-term goal to accept totally
that whatever happens is for our eternal spiritual welfare.

We may find that we already have two kinds of
consciousness. We observe that IT (our proprium) is very
anxious about many things: time, space, money, reputation,
meetings, and so forth. And yet, we also may have a slight
awareness that, although our proprium is untrusting, *we are not
our proprium* and that another, higher part of us *does* trust in
divine providence.

At one of my son's wrestling matches, a part of me was *very* concerned about what the outcome would be. But another, higher part of me could watch that first part of me and know that no matter what happened, the outcome would be the best for the eternal welfare of my son and everyone else. Certainly, if your child were playing in a sports event and you had to choose between (1) your child winning and the win taking away from his or her eternal welfare or (2) your child losing and the loss benefiting your child eternally, you would say, "Please, let my child lose."

That is the way it actually is; whatever does happen is for everyone's eternal spiritual welfare. There is part of us that can trust in that fact. It isn't that we don't have IT that is determined and obsessed; it is just that we need not place the feeling of who we are in that proprium or in the experience IT is having.

We want to live our lives *in* the world, but not *of* the world. We have to operate in the world, but nonetheless we can at the same time be somewhat separated from the world as we live, think, and act from higher states.

In the Work, a lot of emphasis is placed on "being here now," on being present and conscious. You might ask, "Well, in a tense situation, where is it that I am supposed to be?"

Suppose that you are on your way to the airport and your car is running out of gas or that you are playing in a basketball game and the score is very close. Time is running short, and the question is whether you are supposed to be anxious about getting to the airport on time or nervous about how the game will turn out. Is that anxiety the place or state you are meant to be in right now?

No. It is not a matter of exactly where we are, but of elevating our thinking. Swedenborg's writings say that to elevate our thinking is to not only look to the eternal and realize that the Lord is taking care of us, but also to look down and notice what is going on in the physical, natural world. We are to have a double experience.

We may enjoy going to sporting events. It is fascinating to watch the crowd's involvement go back and forth, to participate in the yelling and screaming, while you are having an awareness that it is people's ITs that are doing all that yelling and screaming.

We are capable of much more than our usual behavior, however. We are capable of enjoying our team winning while not getting over-excited about the victory. We can avoid getting upset if our team loses and still care and want our team to win.

To maintain the double awareness, we must not identify with the self, our selfish proprium. Our proprium will, of course, be very caught up in the concerns of time and space. But the more we can pull the feeling of who we are away from those concerns, the more we can come into a state of trust and peace.

The truth is that we need not be run by our propriums. We all remember the depth of despair at losing and the momentous joy of winning. Winning and losing were once everything. Now, we can go to events and give ourselves permission to cheer for the winners and be slightly upset for the losers, but it is not the same state as it used to be before we came to know our devious propriums. We don't want to become cold and aloof from everything. We still want to participate, but without setting our hearts on the outcome. Now we can also be happy about someone else's winning. We can see other competing athletes as human beings rather than as the enemy. We now realize that the people cheering for the other team are just people who also have ITs.

You may be asking yourself, "But what about situations that are more spiritual than sports matches? Isn't it appropriate to have strong negative or positive feelings in those situations?"

The answer is "Yes," but we still need to keep a double awareness.

We are talking here about situations in which one of the Ten Commandments is being broken. During a war, perhaps, many innocent people are being killed. When events occur, it is appropriate then to have strong feelings against the forces killing innocent people. But we can still keep an awareness that the Lord is in charge and will bring about good.

The Roles of Effort and Attention

In everyday circumstances, it takes effort and attention to maintain the double awareness of having negative thoughts or feelings, and yet knowing that we are not our proprium. We have to strive consciously to remember the truth of the situation. The effort called for is to elevate our thoughts and allow our feelings also to change. That is what the Work is about: bringing true concepts to common everyday experiences.

So the Work says we should not identify with strong negative emotions. The Work also says that we should not identify with or attribute to ourselves strong positive emotions. We need to be aware that good (loving) thoughts and emotions are from the Lord and that the negative (selfish) ones operate solely through IT.

While at your job one day, you might be thinking, "Tonight I am going to take a long hot bath and then watch my favorite television program." Now you might have that plan in mind, but if you are Working, you must also notice whether you become identified with the plan. At some point does the plan leave off being a thought or a plan and become something you desire so much you can't give it up? You can feel the shift whenever a plan stops being just a plan *and you become the plan.* You set your heart on it. Then, when you come home and someone says, "You can't stay home tonight. We promised to attend our son's classroom conference," you may experience some negative responses. If you haven't identified with the plan, it will be easier to remain separate and flexible because you are holding the plan lightly. Try to become aware of when you make that shift from having a plan to becoming the plan with your heart involved in it.

It is all a matter of "yet not what I want but what you want" (Matthew 26:39). We want to live our lives consciously. Wanting to go home, take a bath, and watch a television show is probably not a very strong desire, but it is an example of a situation in which we can practice being conscious. The more we can stay conscious, the more we will be free from identifying with our self, our plans, our ideas. Then we will be open to letting the Lord lead us and to trusting in him.

We need to see things as they are, see what the truth is. When we see everything from our propriums, using no self-observation and no separation, we *think* we have the experience of seeing things as they are, but that is an illusion. Swedenborg wrote that the proprium is under a cloud of selfish love and love of the world (*Secrets of Heaven* §1047). Because the proprium (or IT) is under a cloud, it cannot see things as they truly are; rather, IT sees things in a perverted, warped way.

As we withdraw from our proprium and look down at our life from higher thoughts or truths, we come closer and closer to seeing things objectively. For example, as we observe ourselves closely, we may find that we lie more often than we thought, or that we have feelings of contempt for others more often than we realized. As a result of observation we come a little closer to seeing how things are and always have been with us.

In the AA program or a drug treatment program, when someone admits that he is powerless, then change is possible. Although the truth or seeing things can bring about change, the self, of course, doesn't want to be seen! IT lies and rationalizes and pretends it is not lying, and under those conditions the truth cannot have much of an impact on us. So, it is very important to bring truth to our active states. When you refuse to see the truth you are murdering the truth, even though what you are murdering is the very thing that can bring about your freedom and a change.

Seeing the truth about our real nature is what brings about the change. If we deny it, we are killing the very truth that the Lord is trying to reveal to us, which is the truth about our self. The Lord uses temptation to bring that nature up to our awareness.

When we get to the point of choosing some states and rejecting others, we have made progress. In *Secrets of Heaven* §1079, Swedenborg describes people who are in charity and those who are not. We can interpret this passage as describing charitable and uncharitable states within you and within me. We can each recognize such states in ourselves if we are willing to observe them:

> Those who have faith that inheres in charity . . . notice the good [in a person], and if they do see evil or falsity they excuse it, and if possible, labor with that person to correct it. . . . Where charity does not exist, self-love is present and consequently hatred toward all who do not show favor to oneself. As a result they see in the neighbor nothing except that neighbor's evil. If they do see anything good, they either perceive it as nothing, or they place a bad interpretation on it. . . . With those who have no charity, a feeling of hatred radiates from every pore. They wish to try everyone, and indeed to pass judgment on them. Their one desire is to discover what is evil in them, all the time having it in mind to condemn, punish, and torment. But those who have charity hardly notice the evil in another person, but instead notice everything good and true in the person.

So, we want to observe carefully those states in us that are continually having hatred for the neighbor, looking for their errors, wishing to condemn them and talk behind their back. We want to separate from those states and realize they are not Real I. Likewise, we want to become sensitive to the kinds of states that are much finer and truly charitable. Loving states that are able to really appreciate another person, that are capable of looking at people positively, presuming goodness in them—such states have a very different feeling to them than negative I states.

When you go to a sports event like a football or baseball game, study the competition until you get a feeling for the humanness and goodness that is present. There is humanness and goodness present even in the parent of the child competing with your own child. Get a feeling for the love that other parent has for their child. It is there, but you have to consciously seek to be aware of it.

Evil thoughts come to us easily. They press and want to impose themselves on us. Good thoughts, on the other hand, may have to be asked for or sought after. They don't impose themselves on us, and they are much finer and more sensitive. We cannot find them in the same way as the evil thoughts because the good thoughts will not be competing in the same loud voice. The good thoughts will be quieter, gentler, and different.

Notice the difference between these kinds of states within you. Make a choice as to which you want near and which you allow to flow through you out into the world.

Incoming Impressions

In the Work, an "incoming impression" is anything we are aware of (or are impressed by) from the outside world, anything that comes to us through the senses. When we notice that it's snowing outside the window, for example, we are having an "incoming impression." Other examples are the music playing on the radio or the way a friend has changed her hairstyle: when you notice it, it is an "incoming impression."

The Work talks about impressions as if they are food. There is regular food that we digest, and then it turns into bone and muscle, etc. And there is air as a food that is taken in and becomes part of our blood and goes to all our cells, including those of the brain, to feed them. The third kind of food is "incoming impressions," and these include the programs we watch on television, the papers we read, the people to whom we talk.

Let's consider the last kind of food and its effects on us. There are many kinds of pollution today. Our cities, waterways, and even the air we breathe are polluted.

Of course, there are different levels of pollution. A broken television or an old bed mattress just thrown in the creek is certainly one level of pollution. Another level might be the dumping of noxious chemicals into the stream. If you go out to get your trash can and notice that there are a couple of pieces of paper that got free and are still blowing around, you may decide, "I don't want to bother trying to catch those." Each kind of pollution has its own effect on the environment as it is let loose on the world.

Some pollution is taken in by us. We know that if we eat bad food or breathe bad air, we will get sick. Negative incoming impressions can also have a bad effect on us.

And even though the most important thing in our spiritual lives is how we react, we are still responsible for what we put out into the universe because everything we do impacts other people. Pollution on the natural level, in our physical world, is careless at best and inhumane at the worst. And that is just as true of pollution on the spiritual level. Unless we use conscious effort and attention, we pollute the spiritual atmosphere with our unthinking, uncaring, hostile, negative thoughts and emotions.

We can to some degree become conscious of what impact our words have on other people. For example, if we meet someone we don't like and later talk to a third person about the first person, we would be giving a negative impression out into the world, and it would have a polluting impact. We are constantly putting out impressions. What kind of impressions are we creating? Ones that are good for the atmosphere, good for other people? Or are we creating impressions that continue to keep up a feeling of futility or animosity, a feeling that everything is unpleasant, unfortunate, or even evil? What is the impression and what is the impact? What thoughts and feelings are coming through us and manifesting themselves in the external world through us?

The Lord's Prayer states, "Your kingdom come, Your will be done, on earth as in heaven" (Matthew 6:10). But right now there is hell on earth. If you don't believe that, just open your daily paper. Read, and you will find that ten-year-old children are killing nine-year-old children. You will find that mothers are killing babies. So, hellish influences appear to rule.

The Lord's kingdom will not come without people's cooperation. The Lord *can* come through us and then onto the earth; it is our choice which influences (good or bad) we share with the world around us. As we observe our propriums, we may not be able to change them, but there are things that we can refuse to let out into the universe, such as negative feelings or negative, critical remarks. We can become aware of doing these things and probably do less. They may not seem to be very important faults when you are just talking to someone at work or to a neighbor, and you make some negative comment, or maybe just raise your eyebrows. You may not consider that pollution, but the cumulative effect *is* spiritual pollution.

One way to avoid certain kinds of polluting is to stay with "I statements" when talking with others. If you say, for example, "I feel upset," this statement is different from the statement "So-and-so upsets me." The first is a simple statement of fact, while the second is pollution.

Similarly, if you were talking about someone else and said, "I think so-and-so has a good idea for solving a problem," that is different from saying "So-and-so has a good idea for solving a problem." In the first instance, you didn't say that the person definitely has a good idea, just that you think that they do. No one can quarrel with a statement of your opinion, and no one can mistake it for a fact.

IT's mechanical, unthinking way of talking about our neighbor is starting to be obvious. We have to become more conscious of pollution and the fact that we are doing the polluting.

Separating from Specific Evils

If after observing ourselves, we notice that we lie a lot, that is a shock to our systems.

Both the Work and Swedenborg's writings talk about "coming to loathe the self." The Work even speaks about the "terror of the situation."

Now, at our stage of observation, we have become somewhat disquieted, but perhaps we are not yet at the loathing or terror stage. However, more and deeper observation will show us that the self we are looking at is not just different from what we had supposed and it is not just not quite as good as we had thought: *IT is bad.* IT is, in fact, practically ruling our entire lives, hurting the people we love.

And IT has no wish to let us go. Even breaking little habits is difficult. But don't wait till you are ready to break away in big ways. It is impossible to change all at once, and the Lord does all the real work. It is not just a matter of our moving away from evil, anyway; IT is holding on to us! In fact, the Lord is competing with IT for our eternal life.

The more we observe ourselves, the more we see specific evils in our thoughts and feelings, the more shocks we will have. That is good because the shocks act like a sledge hammer hitting a wall, and our former view of ourselves as one solid person becomes instead a different view of a lot of little loves and impulses, and as many, many little negative feelings to which we can apply the truth. Through examination, just like with a wall, we see smaller pieces we can work on, letting water like truth soak into specific cracks.

Claiming we are evil from head to toe doesn't do any good. We have to get into the very specifics, like noticing that we are about to say something negative and instead applying the truth, controlling what comes out of our mouths. That is really doing something.

You might be sitting in your kitchen gossiping about somebody and all of a sudden that very person walks through your kitchen door. You might get a red flush in the face and wonder if she heard you. You find she didn't hear, and then you are suddenly sweet and include her in the conversation. But if you took that shock, if you really looked at yourself and saw that you are not the nice person you pretend to be, that you are a gossip, then that is taking the shock. It will make a difference, a big positive difference.

As a federal probation officer, I use tape recorders and cameras to record conversations with my clients about their crimes. These recordings and films are played later in open court. If you want to see people going through a shock about who they are, that is one place to do it.

The shocks are good examples for us and very beneficial to us. When we have a miserable day and our behavior is hideous, we must remember that beating up on ourselves is not the answer to improvement. Self-hatred is of no use at all, whereas seeing the state objectively is very useful. We will get to see our states more and more clearly if we try to be observant about them.

Although the Work seems difficult and we see unpleasant things about ourselves, the result saves us from our captive relationship to IT. Mercifully, the Lord does not make us see things fully, all at once, because if we did see everything at once we could not stand it.

Some people pollute, but others pick up the trash. And some people not only pick up the trash, but they also like to plant gardens and trim trees, and do other wonderful things. There is a tremendous difference between polluting and doing these other things, not only to you and me, but to everyone.

The following quote from Swedenborg's *Spiritual Experiences* (§5796) discusses how the Lord leads us toward choosing to act with goodness and to avoid spiritual pollution:

> The inner core of real Christians . . . is . . . turned toward heaven. The Lord guides their will . . . and gives them a desire for good, or in other words the ability to be touched by good, or

to rejoice in it. He also guides their intellect so that it can be
affected by truth. The moment they hear something true, they
rejoice in it, and it takes root in their life. The more truth they
learn, the more truth they have inside them, and the Lord leads
them by means of it. . . . We are led by means of what we know.
The Lord acts on the things we know and in the process gives
direction to our feelings and thoughts. . . . The goal is not for us
to look at truth and think, "Now I will graft this onto my life."
To do this would be to act from proprium. Instead, the Lord
leads us by means of what we learn with affection or love.

A person is not to take a truth and decide that she is going
to change her life with it. Why not? Because if someone were
to do that, she would be acting from her proprium (or IT). The
proprium often decides to change its life to be better, even to
be perfect, from now on. However, the proprium cannot
succeed, because only the Lord can change our inner lives.
That's why Swedenborg tells us in *True Christianity* §576 that
the Lord's activity is in the person's passivity. When we
become passive and *allow* the Lord to change us, it is an
entirely different situation from attempting to change ourselves
on our own. We cannot change ourselves.

Trying to grow spiritually by ourselves just doesn't work.
Only the Lord can act. Maybe the proprium (or IT) seems to
be trying to do what the Lord wants, but IT is acting as if it
could succeed by itself, which is spiritual theft. We have only
the ability to observe or examine our behavior, and when we
see our behavior clearly enough to be willing to have it
changed by the Lord, then in his own time he will change our
behavior for us.

The Work says that, when we really observe something, it
no longer has power over us. And once we really see that we
have nothing to contribute but observation, the Lord can come
through us. Other than observation, we actually have nothing
to contribute except love of self, the usual state of humankind.

When our selfish I is active, it is one hundred percent evil. But if we can separate from a selfish I, the Lord does come through us.

We can trust the Lord. Children are ignorant and helpless. They are willing to take their parent's hand and be led. When their mother or father is driving the car on a long trip, children are often asleep in the back seat or playing a game, trusting their parents to care for them. Not only are the children trusting, but the parents, if wise, are trusting their Heavenly Father.

We have to come to a state where we consciously and from understanding recognize that we are helpless and are willing to take the Lord's hand and be led. We can trust and know the Lord is in charge.

> A voice says, "Cry out!"
>   And I said, "What shall I cry?"
> All people are grass,
>   Their constancy is like the flower of the field. . . .
> The grass withers, the flower fades;
>   But the word of our God will stand forever.
> Get you up to a high mountain,
>   O Zion, herald of good tidings;
> Lift up your voice with strength,
>   O Jerusalem, herald of good tidings.
>   Lift it up, do not fear.
>   — Isaiah 40:6–9

To grow spiritually, we have to continually allow the old part of us, our old negative I's, to die, because we automatically want to give in to them, to revive them.

Eventually, many things we give up now will be returned to us, but after they are cleansed of negativity. Until then, our good and bad I's are so intermingled that we have to Work on separation, and this is scary. A part of us knows we can't go back to the way we were before we started Working. After we have been observing for a while and we see how much damage our negative I's do, a part of us won't want to return to the negative I's, no matter how pleasing it may seem at certain times.

The Task for Chapter 14

"Sense" whenever you are talking to someone about another person.

Recall that "sensing" is putting your attention to or pressing a spot on your hand, until you have awareness of warmth or other sensation in that spot, and then maintaining the sensation by means of continued attention. The purpose of "sensing" is to avoid giving your full attention to a negative state or behavior or to prevent that negative state or behavior. "Sensing" can also be a sign of willingness to Work.

We may know that we have an inclination to gossip, but if we do the task, we will become more aware of it than in the past. Mechanically we may be talking about another person, but sensing will help us observe what is going on and may increase our effort to stay awake. When we fall asleep, we are totally identified with negative states and then evil can operate through us, so we want to stay conscious of potential evil.

When we talk to someone about another person, we are in danger of becoming negative, in danger of polluting the spiritual atmosphere. It is wise to start sensing before we start talking about anyone, rather than to try and recover after catching ourselves gossiping. So, whenever you start a conversation that is going to include talk about someone who is not present, sense while talking.

When the task refers to talking about a "person," that means a person you know well, a person you know somewhat, or a person totally unknown to you, like a movie star or someone mentioned in the newspaper. You may be guarded or careful when discussing someone you know well, but find yourself expressing contempt for a rock star or politician, even though you don't know the person at all.

You can also silently ask yourself, while sensing, "What is the impact of what I am saying? What am I putting out into the world?" Maybe no one will even notice a metaphorical cigarette butt being thrown onto the trail, but if you are doing it, then be aware of doing it. Observe.

We do not need to change anything at this time. You are not being asked *not* to talk about another person; rather, you are being asked not to pollute with negative statements or impressions. I am just asking you to *sense while talking* so that you become more aware and conscious. Just sense your hand by pressing a spot or holding your hand in a different way, or whatever works for you, as a reminder to be aware as you talk about another person.

You may find that sensing helps you to have a good impact or impression on someone instead of a negative impact. You may find that you have a good influence.

CHAPTER 15
Establishing a New Viewpoint

Where your consciousness is, there you are.

— *Maurice Nicoll*

Omni magazine printed an article on how to have a mystical experience. Here is an excerpt:

Mystical experiences are not necessarily extraordinary events that happen only to extraordinary people such as dedicated meditators or peyote eaters. You may deliberately induce a mystical state by paying attention to subtle feelings and ideas lying just beneath the layers of everyday awareness. That is what mystics and gurus have been telling people for thousands of years. Quite simply, begin to notice—in a non-judgmental way—how you talk about your life, rationalize your behavior, explain the world around you. By shifting your awareness from mundane concerns and temporarily suspending your "belief systems," you may be more ready to experience life from the vantage point of the sage. You may even feel connected to something greater than yourself. Your rigid concept of time will probably dissolve into a sense of timelessness, blurring the distinctions between past, present, and future.[1]

---

1. Keith Harary, "How to Have a Mystical Experience," *Omni* 11, no. 3 (December 1988): 137.

If we turn away from the worldly concerns of time and space, we can focus on where causes take place in the spiritual arena. Whether mystical or not, changing our focus like that is turning in the right direction.

The more we look at IT, the more we get a sense of its nature and how impossible it is for us to change by means of our own power. Acknowledging our powerlessness and separating from IT are necessary changes that must take place in us, if we are to grow spiritually. We must become aware of the self, then observe the self, learn not to identify with it, and finally see our true natures and separate from or "die" to the self. All of these are necessary stages we must go through before we can receive from the Lord the states he wishes to give us, states of love to him and love to the neighbor. When we are ready for these, the Lord will give them to us, and we will experience all the joys that come with these states.

The following passage from Swedenborg's *Divine Providence* contrasts love of the neighbor with selfish love. This passage also explains why the Lord allows evil:

> Everyone can see that love for our neighbor and love for ourselves are opposing loves. Love for our neighbor wants to do good to everyone, while love for ourselves wants everyone to be our servants. Love for our neighbor sees all people as our family and friends, while love for ourselves sees all people as our slaves, and if people are not subservient, it sees them as our enemies. In short, it focuses on ourselves alone and sees others as scarcely human. At heart it values them no more than our horses and dogs, and since it regards them as basically worthless, it thinks nothing of doing them harm. . . . These are the evils to which we are prone from birth . . . [but] evil is permitted for the purpose of salvation.
>
> — *Divine Providence* §276[b]

When we are in an evil state, or when we are experiencing evil emotions and thoughts, we often think that we should not be having such thoughts or experiences and that if we were good people we would not be having them. However, the Lord allows evils to appear in us, to come before us. In fact, it is very important that each of us goes through the stage of seeing our evils.

When we first begin to Work, we find out that we are asleep. When we can feel separation, that is ideal; but when we can't, at least we can observe and know what is going on. We can say, "IT is angry" or "IT is envious." We can just observe the experience.

The Lord may be giving us an experience of anger or other negative state to let us know how serious it is and how serious he is about wanting to help us! This isn't just for our entertainment. The Lord is trying to save our eternal lives from hell.

Seeing our evils is what begins to break our dependence on our own intelligence (when we should instead be relying upon the Lord's guidance) and starts our spiritual transition away from selfish loves toward love of the neighbor and the Lord.

Trusting during Difficult Times

There is a painting of the disciples in a boat on the rough sea, with the Lord standing above them on the waves. The Lord obviously is there to protect the disciples. What is not so obvious is that he is the one who created the sea and allowed the storm to happen in the first place.

It appeared to the disciples that the Lord was not even with them during the storm. But the Lord was there. And he is present now, with everything that happens, even in our experiences that appear to be negative. Everything is under his control, and even the negative elements are being used for good by him.

If we stay as awake as we can, our relationship to the Lord will change. We can truly love someone only when we experience him and know him personally. This is as true for loving the Lord as it is for loving human beings. When we have negative states that are interfering in our lives but then we experience the Lord doing something for us to change that, from the new experiences we can *feel* love toward the Lord rather than *thinking* about loving the Lord or feeling we *should* be loving the Lord. When we experience him trying to save us from a hellish life, then a new love for him is born.

But we must stay awake in order to see what he is saving us from. And when he seems to withdraw a little and let us go into a negative state, he is just letting us know how much he loves us. And that is when we need to Work hardest.

What work can we do? Perhaps we can only "sense," or "stop thought." Just know that it is time to Work. When we Work, truth starts to give us goodness.

The Lord wishes to give us peace to replace the anger; he wishes to give us joy or hope to replace the sadness. He wishes to give us new closeness or acceptance. He wants to give us the opposite of whatever negative we are experiencing, and that's why he is present.

It all becomes very real if we are willing to Work. Working is not just an intellectual exercise. Working is a real experience.

King Nebuchadnezzar, the most powerful king in the world at the time, had a dream about a tree. The tree had beautiful leaves and spreading branches where birds nested, and animals grazed beneath it (Daniel 4:10–12).

In the dream, a messenger from heaven came and said to cut down the tree, but to leave the stump in the field where there was dew. And although the tree was cut down to a stump, there was still some potential for something new to grow again.

After waking, King Nebuchadnezzar asked Daniel what the tree in his dream meant, and Daniel said, "It is you."

Then the tragedy that occurred in the dream happened to Nebuchadnezzar in another way in his waking life. Suddenly, he went insane, and rather than acting as a powerful king, he went raving out in the fields where rain drenched him, and he became so hungry he ate grass (Daniel 4:33).

When King Nebuchadnezzar was returned home again, sane, he realized that the experience of being out in the wild taught him something he never could have learned otherwise. When he was first king, he had thought he really was the mighty king, but his misfortunes showed him that kingship was something that was never really his at all, that it was something the Lord could give and could also take away. There was only one real King, and that is the Lord:

> When that period was over, I, Nebuchadnezzar, lifted my eyes to heaven, and my reason returned to me.
> I blessed the Most High,
>   and praised and honored the one who lives forever.
> For his sovereignty is an everlasting sovereignty,
>   and his kingdom endures from generation to generation.
> — Daniel 4:34

That living belief changed King Nebuchadnezzar. No one told him that truth; no one instructed him. It was a living experience that brought about his new state.

An Appearance of Power

Have you ever heard a little child of four or five years suddenly announce, "I can do it myself!"? A little girl just barely able to walk pushes off from the couch and starts to walk toward her mom. Her mom holds her arms out, and the little girl suddenly turns a different way, as if saying, "Now I can go wherever I want!" That happens at some point. And when children get older, they can drive the car, have a summer job, buy some of their own clothes, and so forth. The appearance is that they are becoming more powerful, and their self-determination increases. When they marry and have their own family, their self-determination increases even more.

We do not teach very young people about the Work. One reason is that first they should develop their own personalities.

After they become adults, perhaps they start to feel that there is more to life than possessions. At a time such as this, they can begin to look inward and open up to new ideas. They may be ready to learn about the Work.

Early in a person's life, he experiences the appearance of his own increasing power. But eventually, if a person is to grow spiritually, his self-determination has to be broken.

We can read about the nature of divine providence, but even if we believe it intellectually, our belief will tend to go away again. If our own will is broken by experience and our own selfish loves are shaken loose, then our states really change.

Divine providence will always give us some things we cannot control. It might be our children, it might be our moods or health, or our drinking. *Everyone eventually gets the experience of not being in control.* First it may be an external event, as when a chief executive has a heart attack. While in the hospital, he gets out of the bed. The nurse says, "Mr. Smith, get back in bed!" The big executive says, "Do you know who I am? I am the chief executive of the Sitcom Corporation." The nurse says, "Here, you aren't. Here you are just a patient. Get back in bed!" At that point, the patient realizes that there are certain things he cannot control. That is a very good thing to have happen because it starts his spiritual transition. The experience of not being in control softens something that has to be softened if spiritual progress is to be made.

When a child decides she is finally going to be her own boss, she tells her mom that everyone has to stay out of her room; it is *her* room. She decides she is going to fix her own breakfast and be totally independent. The parent may go along with this and allow the child that experience, but of course "*her* room" happens to be in the house purchased by the parents, and all the furniture in the child's room was bought by the parents. All of her clothes were purchased by the parents, too. When the child goes to make her breakfast, it is to their refrigerator, to their milk and cereal, to their bowl, to make *her* breakfast.

And that is about our position in relation to the Lord's providence.

It just looks as if we are in charge. This body of ours is one we did not make, and we certainly do not know how to manage it from minute to minute or day to day. We don't even know where our thoughts come from most of the time, and we don't know how they attach to our emotions or even how our hearts beat or how our lungs operate in detail. And yet, like the child, we feel we can handle our own lives.

Before a child comes into a state where there is an appearance of power, the child was in innocence, totally willing to be led. But as the child grows, he or she comes out of that state.

As men and women, we have to work toward consciously returning to an earlier state of innocence and a willingness to be led, but this time with an acknowledgment that the Lord provides everything. Swedenborg discusses the result of this spiritual journey toward renewed innocence:

> When [people convinced of their own purity] are brought into a particular state in order that they may perceive hell within themselves, and perceive this so clearly as to despair of the possibility of their own salvation, . . . for the first time . . . their pride and their contempt for all others in comparison with themselves [is broken down]. . . . They can now be brought into a true confession of faith, not merely to the confession that all good comes from the Lord but also that all things exist because of His mercy; and at length they can be brought into humility of heart before the Lord, the existence of which is impossible without acknowledgement of what they are in themselves.
> —*Secrets of Heaven* §2694[4]

We must look deeper into the difference between appearances and reality. When we are living our lives from the proprium, in the love of self and concerned about the world, we are in appearances. The world is not as it seems because the causes of our internal states are not to be found in external occurrences, although it appears as if our internal states originate there.

For instance, it often appears to us that an external event causes our negative emotion. If you are driving down the road on your way to a show and one of your tires goes flat, it will appear as if that flat tire caused you to be angry, upset, or irritable. There is also the appearance that people can cause a negative emotion. Let's say you fix your tire and resume; as you come around the corner, a farmer in an old truck pulls out in front of you going twenty miles an hour in the sixty mile-an-hour zone. It appears as if that farmer is causing your impatience. It also seems as if time and space have something to do with your negative emotions. *I want to get to that show by 8:30 p.m. If the farmer were behind, I wouldn't mind.*

The Work says that, when we are in a negative state and are operating from appearances, we might think that we can solve our problem on the same level as the appearance. IT thinks, "As long as I can get to the show by 8:30, I won't be upset."

The Work, however, teaches that negative states cannot be fixed on the natural level, because our emotions are not caused by the external world. Our emotions are caused by our internal world. If we try to change a negative state on the natural plane, the state may leave temporarily, only to return sooner or later, probably in response to some new event that occurs in the external world. The only way we can truly address a negative state is on the spiritual level, by Working on ourselves, by observing ourselves. To be subdued, negative states must be addressed on the spiritual plane.

There is really only one question to be asked when we are in a negative state: *What is it the Lord wants me to look at right now?* If you have a flat tire and are angry, the question to ask yourself is not about the tire or the time but only *What does the Lord want me to look at?* And the answer, of course, is that he wants us to look at the negative state that is with us, at that state of anger or frustration, at our feelings and thoughts, at where we are spiritually at that moment.

If we are looking at events from a negative emotion, IT (our proprium) will lie. If we are in a negative emotion, any thought, any internal monologue in our heads is, at least partially, a lie. In some situations, IT will say, "Oh, you are so stupid. You always make a mistake!" Well, that is a lie because you do not *always* make mistakes. If IT says that someone else is this or that, it is a lie, because nobody is *only* this or that.

If you are in a negative state and are talking to someone, you can be sure that whatever you are saying is, in some way, a lie. Also, if someone else is in a negative state, and he speaks to you about a third party, you can listen intently to what he says and hear what is false about it. You might, of course, hear something that is not factually correct, an obvious lie. However, what if the person says something that is indeed a fact? Perhaps the person in a negative state says that Sam is an alcoholic. If Sam is an alcoholic, where is the lie? In this case, the lie is not in the fact but in the negative emotion. For instance, there is an implication that the fact that Sam is an alcoholic justifies a feeling of contempt for him. However, it is a lie. *There is no fact that justifies a feeling of contempt toward another person.* A feeling of contempt is a lie, even if what is said is factually true.

A hateful emotion has no justification to exist regardless of the facts.

If we can see what is untrue in what we think, our belief in the lie will go away. If we can see the thought that supports the negative feeling, then the thought and the feeling will lose their power over us.

But we need to realize that there are different kinds of falsehoods. There are certain states that are so blatantly untrue we immediately reject their claims. Those are the easy ones. The tough ones are those we may need to observe for years before we can see how they are untrue.

Here is an example. When I am having negative feelings or thoughts about a person who lives immorally, I may feel not only justified but perhaps that it's appropriate or even helpful. I

think, "It serves him right that I disapprove of him." The
thoughts that the person should know better or be living
differently make me feel right or better than that person. But
this is a pleasure from hell, an evil delight and untrue. The lie
or false thinking is that I am better than he and that his evil
should be attributed to him and that any goodness in me is
mine. It may take years before we recognize how false such
automatic attitudes are.

People ask, "What should I do?" The first answer is "Just
observe." Later, when we are not identified, when we can look
at ourselves with non-judgmental, non-critical observation and
separation, then perhaps we will be in a state in which the
Lord can be active in us. For now, it is important to observe,
and if you can, or need to, "sense" while observing.

Growing through Observing

What does observation lead to? It leads to more observation.

Eventually, of course, after enough observation over a long
enough period of time, we may be able not to identify with
negative emotions and thoughts. We still observe ourselves, but
now we are beginning to feel that we are not IT. Separation
starts to take place, and we can see the true nature of IT.

So, observation leads to selfish loves becoming quiescent and
love of the Lord, or the Lord within you, becoming active. But
it all starts with observation, observation, observation.

If I took someone to a nearby forest and said, "Today I want
you to observe the forest," the person might observe it. If the
next day I took her to the same place and said, "Today you are
going to observe the forest," she might say, "I did that
yesterday." But I might say, "This time I want you to only
observe leaves. Oak leaves, maple leaves, different colors,
different shapes, observe all the leaves." The next day I might
take the person to the same place and say, "Today we are going
to observe the forest again. Especially observe the different
barks on the trees. Observe what color a bark is on the south

side and again on the north side, etc., etc." I could take a person to that forest one thousand days in a row, and each day I could specify something different to be observed in that forest.

Our negative emotions are like the trees and bark and leaves in a big forest. There are many things to observe when we Work. Some days we look at contempt; other days we look at lying. Observation can go on indefinitely, getting more and more detailed.

Noncritical, nonjudgmental observation is what is needed. We can't observe something if we keep looking away from it. If we look away because we want something to be different than it is, we will never see the actual particulars of it.

Imagine that someone shoots you in the arm and the ambulance brings you to the hospital emergency room. Your arm is bleeding profusely. Now suppose that the emergency-room doctor comes up to you, looks at your wound, and then hides his eyes with his hands. You would yell, "Help! Get me another doctor! I want someone to look at this!" In contrast, if a doctor arrived who had treated soldiers in a war and after a good look at your arm the doctor said, "You'll be all right," you would feel that this doctor would attend to your arm with whatever attention was needed and that you would indeed be okay.

Our self-observation needs to be just as attentive and nonjudgmental as a doctor's observation in the emergency room.

You are trying to observe your proprium, and you want to know IT in detail so that eventually you can separate from it. You need to know IT in detail, not in general, in order to gain separation.

Swedenborg wrote that it would be much easier for people to grow spiritually if they would not attribute good or evil to themselves (*Divine Providence* §320). As soon as we realize we are looking at our proprium and not our true selves, then we will no longer feel we need to justify or defend the negatives that IT thinks or feels. When we gain separation, we will have no need to wish that things in our lives could be different than they are. When a negative state occurs, we will be able just to look at it and not judge it, and we will be able to learn from it whatever we can.

You may be wondering how examining our negative states can lead us to peaceful (or good) states. The answer has to do with the nature of truth and good and is illustrated by the story of the manna given to the Israelites. When the Israelites were in the desert, the Lord sent them meat in the evenings and manna in the mornings:

> . . . in the morning there was a layer of dew around the camp. When the layer of dew lifted, there on the surface of the wilderness was a fine flaky substance, as fine as frost on the ground. When the Israelites saw it, they said to one another, "What is it?" For they did not know what it was. Moses said to them, "It is the bread that the LORD has given you to eat. This is what the LORD has commanded: 'Gather as much of it as each of you needs. . .'"
>
> The house of Israel called it manna; it was like coriander seed, white, and the taste of it was like wafers made with honey. . . . The Israelites ate manna forty years, until they came to a habitable land; they ate manna, until they came to the border of the land of Canaan.　　—Exodus 16:13–16; 31, 35

The manna the Lord sent was white, and it tasted sweet, "like wafers made with honey." According to Swedenborg, on a spiritual level, the manna the Lord sent was like the joining of truth and good in a peaceful state (*Secrets of Heaven* §8511).

So how does the story about manna relate to our Working toward peaceful states? As we observe our negative thoughts and feelings, we are looking at the truth about our lives. We see each negative state for what it truly is, and because we see more spiritual truth about our lives, the Lord helps us to live better. During this process, our love of truth becomes more active. New pleasures or perceptions come to us every day as a result of living our lives from the truths we see about ourselves.

Our new good states and perceptions don't come from out there in the world: they come from turning around and looking within. The new states are the manna we receive from the Lord after we Work. The manna is the Lord in our lives. He is always there, and we will receive good and peaceful states from him as we see more and more spiritual truth about our lives.

The Task for Chapter 15

When you are negative, keep asking the question, *What does the Lord wish me to look at?*

If you suddenly become angry, upset, sad, impatient, jealous, or irritated, ask this question, and then ask it again. He is giving you this experience, so there must be something that he wishes you to notice.

Our natural minds want to avoid unpleasant experiences, to just get out of the negativity or away from the person who seems to be causing the problem. Our natural minds want the situation to be different from what it actually is. But what does the Lord want me to get out of this experience? Keep asking that question until you have a clear idea of what it is in each event or situation that he wants you to see.

Whatever your spiritual state, you can Work, and the Lord will draw you closer to heaven.

ADDITIONAL READING

There are many books that can assist in efforts toward spiritual growth. The books listed below are especially helpful in clarifying the steps of transformation and inspiring the reader to start living a more conscious life of awareness at once.

Bennett, John. *Witness*. Charles Town, W. Va.: Claymont Communications, 1983.
   The autobiography of John Bennett's fascinating life as a dedicated follower and confidante of Gurdjieff and Ouspensky and friend to other spiritual leaders of his time. An amazing example of what is possible through the Work.

Nicoll, Maurice. *Psychological Commentaries on the Teaching of Gurdjieff & Ouspensky*. Boulder, Colo.: Shambhala Publications, Inc., 1984. [Currently published by Red Wheel/Weiser.]
   This five-volume study from lectures by Nicoll is an in-depth presentation of the "Work" concepts, explaining the relationship between personality and essence and how to work on yourself.

Ouspensky, P.D. *The Fourth Way*. New York: Vantage Books Random House, 1971.
   Compiled by his students from more than twenty-five years of his lectures, this book covers every facet of the theory on humankind's possible evolution. Written in a question-and-answer format.

————. *In Search of the Miraculous*. Orlando, Fla.: Harcourt Brace & Co., 2001.
   Ouspensky's personal search for the truth. A thorough study of the Work and its methods of change as taught to him (orally) by Gurdjieff.

Rose, Frank, and Robert Maginal. *The Joy of Spiritual Growth: Real Encounters.* West Chester, Pa.: The Swedenborg Foundation, 1999.

This book also presents a spiritual-growth seminar, based on the Work and the writings of Emanuel Swedenborg, as taught by Peter Rhodes.

BIBLIOGRAPHY OF WORKS BY EMANUEL SWEDENBORG

Apocalypse Explained. 6 vols. Translated by John Whitehead. 2nd ed. West Chester, Pa.: The Swedenborg Foundation, 1994–1998.

Apocalypse Revealed. 2 vols. Translated by John Whitehead. 2nd ed. West Chester, Pa.: The Swedenborg Foundation, 1997.

A new translation of this work, to be entitled *Revelation Unveiled,* will be available from the NEW CENTURY EDITION OF THE WORKS OF EMANUEL SWEDENBORG in the near future.

Arcana Coelestia. 12 vols. Translated by John Clowes. Revised by John F. Potts. 2nd ed. West Chester, Pa.: The Swedenborg Foundation, 1995–1998. The first volume of this work is also available under the title *Heavenly Secrets.*

A new translation of this work, to be entitled *Secrets of Heaven,* will be available from the NEW CENTURY EDITION OF THE WORKS OF EMANUEL SWEDENBORG in the near future.

Charity: The Practice of Neighborliness. Translated by William F. Wunsch. Edited by William R. Woofenden. West Chester, Pa.: The Swedenborg Foundation, 1995.

Conjugial Love. Translated by Samuel S. Warren. Revised by Louis Tafel. 2nd ed. West Chester, Pa.: The Swedenborg Foundation, 1998. This volume is also available under the title *Love in Marriage,* translated by David Gladish, 1992.

A new translation of this work, to be entitled *Marriage Love*, will be available from the NEW CENTURY EDITION OF THE WORKS OF EMANUEL SWEDENBORG in the near future.

Divine Love and Wisdom. Translated by John C. Ager. 2nd ed. West Chester, Pa.: The Swedenborg Foundation, 1995.

Divine Love and Wisdom/Divine Providence. Translated by George F. Dole. NEW CENTURY EDITION OF THE WORKS OF EMANUEL SWEDENBORG. West Chester, Pa.: The Swedenborg Foundation, 2003.

Divine Providence. Translated by William Wunsch. 2nd ed. West Chester, Pa.: The Swedenborg Foundation, 1996.

Four Doctrines. Translated by John F. Potts. 2nd ed. West Chester, Pa.: The Swedenborg Foundation, 1997.
    A new translation of the individual volumes of this collection—*The Lord*, *Sacred Scripture*, *Life*, and *Faith*—will be available from the NEW CENTURY EDITION OF THE WORKS OF EMANUEL SWEDENBORG in the near future.

Heaven and Hell. Translated by John C. Ager. 2nd ed. West Chester, Pa.: The Swedenborg Foundation, 1995.

————. Translated by George F. Dole. NEW CENTURY EDITION OF THE WORKS OF EMANUEL SWEDENBORG. West Chester, Pa.: The Swedenborg Foundation, 2000.

The Heavenly City. Translated by Lee Woofenden. West Chester, Pa.: The Swedenborg Foundation, 1993. See also *The New Jerusalem and Its Heavenly Doctrine*, below.

Journal of Dreams. Translated by J. J. G. Wilkinson. Introduction by Wilson Van Dusen. New York: The Swedenborg Foundation,1986. See also *Swedenborg's Dream Diary*.

The Last Judgment in Retrospect. Translated by and edited by
George F. Dole. West Chester, Pa.: The Swedenborg
Foundation, 1996. See also *The Last Judgment and Babylon
Destroyed.*

Miscellaneous Theological Works. Translated by John Whitehead.
2nd ed. West Chester, Pa.: The Swedenborg Foundation,
1996. This volume includes *The New Jerusalem and Its
Heavenly Doctrine, Earths in the Universe,* and *The Last
Judgment* and *Babylon Destroyed,* among others.
　　New translations of the individual titles in this collection
will be available from the NEW CENTURY EDITION OF THE
WORKS OF EMANUEL SWEDENBORG in the near future.

Posthumous Theological Works. 2 vols. Translated by John
Whitehead. 2nd ed. West Chester, Pa.: The Swedenborg
Foundation, 1996. These volumes include the
autobiographical and theological extracts from Swedenborg's
letters, *Additions to True Christian Religion, The Doctrine of
Charity, The Precepts of the Decalogue,* and collected minor
works, among others.

Swedenborg's Dream Diary. Edited by Lars Bergquist. Translated
by Anders Hallengren. West Chester, Pa.: The Swedenborg
Foundation, 2001. See also *Journal of Dreams.*

True Christian Religion. 2 vols. Translated by John C. Ager. 2nd
ed. West Chester, Pa.: The Swedenborg Foundation, 1996.

True Christianity. 2 vols. Translated by Jonathan Rose. NEW
CENTURY EDITION OF THE WORKS OF EMANUEL
SWEDENBORG. West Chester, Pa.: The Swedenborg
Foundation, forthcoming.

Worship and Love of God. Translated by Alfred H. Stroh and
Frank Sewall. 2nd ed. West Chester, Pa.: The Swedenborg
Foundation, 1996.

————. Translated by Stuart Shotwell. New Century Edition
of the Works of Emanuel Swedenborg. West Chester,
Pa.: The Swedenborg Foundation, forthcoming.

Collections of Swedenborg's Writings

*A Compendium of the Theological Writings of Emanuel
Swedenborg.* Translated and edited by Samuel S. Warren.
1875; rpt. New York: Swedenborg Foundation, 1974.

Conversations with Angels: What Swedenborg Heard in Heaven.
Edited by Leonard Fox and Donald Rose. Translated by
David Gladish and Jonathan Rose. West Chester, Pa.:
Chrysalis Books, 1996.

Debates with Devils: What Swedenborg Heard in Hell. Edited by
Donald Rose. Translated by Lisa Hyatt Cooper. West
Chester, Pa.: Chrysalis Books, 2000.

Essential Swedenborg. Edited by Sig Synnestvedt. Rpt. West
Chester, Pa.: The Swedenborg Foundation, 1977.

Poems from Swedenborg. Edited by Leon C. Le Van. New York:
The Swedenborg Foundation, 1987.

A Thoughtful Soul. Translated by and edited by George F. Dole.
West Chester, Pa.: Chrysalis Books, 1995.

Way of Wisdom: Meditations on Love and Service. Edited by
Grant R. Schnarr and Erik J. Buss. West Chester, Pa.:
Chrysalis Books, 1999.